A Local Habitation

A LOCAL HABITATION

Poems from Old & New Worlds

SEABROOK WILKINSON

Charleston London

the
History
PRESS

Published by The History Press
Charleston, SC 29403
www.historypress.net

Cover image: *Porch* by William McCullough. *Courtesy of 53 Cannon Street Gallery. www.williammccullough.com*

First published 2007

Manufactured in the United Kingdom

ISBN 978.1.59629.402.8

Library of Congress Cataloging-in-Publication Data

Wilkinson, Seabrook.
A local habitation : poems from old and new worlds / Seabrook Wilkinson.
p. cm.
ISBN-13: 978-1-59629-402-8 (alk. paper)
1. South Carolina--Poetry. 2. North Carolina--Poetry. 3.
Scotland--Poetry. 4. Mountains--Poetry. I. Title.
PS3623.I5533L63 2007
811'.6--dc22

2007037400

Notice: The information in this book is true and complete to the best of our knowledge. It is offered without guarantee on the part of the author or The History Press. The author and The History Press disclaim all liability in connection with the use of this book.

"After the Fire" first appeared in the 2006 *Kakalak: An Anthology of Carolina Poets.* A number of the other poems made their debuts in the courteous coulmns of the *Charleston Mercury.* Grateful acknowledgement is tendered to both.

For David

Whom words appear to warm,
Dear heart, wear mine.

—James Merrill

The poet's eye, in a fine frenzy rolling,
Doth glance from heaven to earth, from earth to heaven,
And as imagination bodies forth
The forms of things unknown, the poet's pen
Turns them to shapes and gives to airy nothing
A local habitation and a name.

A Midsummer Night's Dream, act V, scene i, lines 12–17

Contents

CONTENTS

CONTENTS

PRELUDE

And I no more
Shall with thee gaze on that unfathomed deep,
The Human Soul—as when, pushed off the shore,
Thy mystic bark would through the darkness sweep,
Itself the while so bright! For oft we seemed
As on some starless sea—all dark above,
All dark below—yet, onward as we drove,
To plough up light that ever round us streamed.

—Washington Allston, "On the Late S.T. Coleridge"

1947

Poor Allston, with his thirty thousand lines,
  Two epics' measure, chalking the immense
Task of adjusting each shadow's confines
  When he dipped the lamp that lit sad pretence
His argosy might ever have sailed. Signs
  Seared Belshazzar's wall, but ego's high fence
Hid truth from the artist. Sick heart cried halt,
And torchlight squired him to the Dana vault. *

Mine was, I am informed, an easy birth:
  Grandfather delivered the longed-for lad,
And every tongue acknowledged Mother's worth.
  Not to chalk life-lines, but what if I had
Assuaged somewhat sooner the heir-male dearth
  Of a storm-pruned tree my advent made glad?
Say, jubilee-year of Bordeaux *Grand Cru*,
In which Dame Blanche also made her début?

Entirely possible, for since the war
  And vows achingly deferred glass had turned
Often enough for an heir, indeed for
  Two, had they been quick. 'Prentice-parents yearned
For triumph in their mission to restore
  Slumped genetic fortunes. Had my lamp burned
A chalk-mark earlier, how much would have changed?
Would all my shadows have been rearranged?

A three-year grade-skip against history—
  My first datable memory would have been
Outbreak of the Korean infamy,
  Not the Coronation's spell-binding screen
(A precocious Royalist, rising three),
  Yet crucial difference not what I'd have seen
Or missed in outer world, but having known
Father before the cancer's fruit had grown.

To have cheered him in health, not as I did,
  Sofa-bound wraith, sunken orbs Calhoun-caped, **
Breath scarce stirring the shroud-like coverlid,
  Firming faith in earthly father who shaped
Green being to his will, who might have bid
  Me realize high dreams that now escaped
His doing, become the surgeon who might
Have saved his poisoned leg by slicing right.

Harvard still, but a very different one,
  Placid, preppy, jacket and tie, all male,
My tenancy's ferment barely begun
  By our overlap year. And then to sail
Across Charles to unwrap the ace surgeon
  Of Father's wish—dodging bullets' hot hail,
Vietnam War then at its most deranged—
Putting right the wrong of a life short-changed.

The standard sequence of residency,
  Fulbright, post-docs, in good time circling back
Home as the man my lost sire meant to be,
  Loving my work, but conscious of sharp lack,
Soul-sapping void, after hours' surgery
  Held late at the office, not to attack
Piled paperwork, but the inarticulate,
Lashed less by passion to cure than create.

For surely something of this tardy son
  Would have dwelt in that firstborn who came not,
Just as in me a soupçon of surgeon
  Flavours the critic. But I nigh forgot
Body's clock's set, that ur-I might have done
  Scalpel's devoir, shrunk to predestined plot,
A fresh-cut face among the time-washed stones
Where Pon Pon eddies past my fathers' bones. ***

* I take liberties in squeezing the final sad score of Washington Allston's years into a single stanza. Walter Channing's estimate of the number of chalk lines and circles was actually twenty thousand. It was in about 1822 that Gilbert Stuart first objected to the perspective of *Belshazzar's Feast*, prompting Allston to lower the central lamp, and fostering self-doubt that slowly killed the project. When the vast canvas was unrolled for the last time in 1839, Allston found further fault with the scale of the main figures. His fevered attempts to redress imbalances were too much for a diseased heart that downed tools towards midnight on Sunday, 9 July 1843. On the following evening his coffin was conducted to the family vault of his second wife, Emily Remington Dana, Harvard undergraduates flanking the procession with torches. Here, in the Burying Ground of the First Congregational Church of Cambridge, he lies a hundred yards west of Harvard Yard, where as an undergraduate between 1796 and 1800 he enjoyed the most carefree years of a greatly troubled life.

** After my father's death, as a slightly older child I somehow came to associate him with the engraving of Calhoun, carried into the Senate chamber on his deathbed, listening as James Murray Mason reads his valedictory speech. Here, as in the bronze likeness dominating Marion Square in Charleston, which Father would have known in his medical college days, the great statesman seems to be gathering Death itself in the heavy cape that envelopes him. A six-year-old would have known that his blood connexion with the Great Nullifier was through the maternal side.

*** Willtown Bluff, on the north bank of the Pon Pon River, as the North Edisto becomes for its final ten sea-seeking miles, has been the preferred place of sepulture of the Wilkinsons of St. Paul's Parish since the opening years of the eighteenth century. Here the immigrant, Captain Christopher Wilkinson, was interred beside the Presbyterian church of which he was long an elder, to be joined later by many of his Anglican descendants. Today the most visible reminders of the site's past are a solitary column of a later church and the imposing table-tomb of William Wilkinson of Summit (1788–1847).

I. Lowcountry

Under the piazza, feet cocked up in the breeze
Coming through dark arcades that uphold his home,
In a royal dalliance from June until Autumn
He airs his feudal fancy richly as he may please.

—Josephine Pinckney, "An Island Boy"

In the Cloakroom with DuBose Heyward

I.P.M. Colonel William Pinckney,
Co-founder of the Charles Town Library Society

Of all that I should miss, most wrenching these—
Not the architectural hordes surge to see,
But the invisible continuities

That web our daily world and ancestry,
Old names and high blood we perpetuate
Without the old serene security,

Sure tenure that moated envied estate—
Mere remnants now, shrinking like highball ice,
Emblems in our own tumblers, come too late

To stoke war with heroic sacrifice,
But not to sup the twilight of our kind,
For there are satisfactions beyond price

Yet to be savoured: At each turn we find
Ourselves filling outlines of vital ghosts,
Latched into pews ours Sundays out of mind,

At hoary founders' feasts proposing toasts
A scroll of sires raised in their long-dimmed day,
Well-pleased no other East-Coast city boasts

A Colonial elite clinging to sway
In church and club, if in other concerns
Obliged—if not quite to yield, to make way.

Rich frisson when a Sully portrait turns,
Eyed by his over-mantel counterpart,
To dance with the pendant for whom he burns.

Of distaffs for these threads, closest to heart
The deep-draft chalice, George II's gift,
Chased marriage of silversmith's and graver's art,

That links our branched blood's lips through every shift
Of fortune and fashion back to the third
Generation native. I never lift

This vessel brimful with incarnate Word
Without I marvel at mystic conjunction
Of lives discreet in time, and, deeply stirred,

Resume our pew nursing fresh-cut compunction
For stumbling stewardship of legacy
Inestimable. But if dud heirs malfunction

At least we have not stooped to "savagery," *
As feared those seventeen young gentlemen
Incorporating a society

To gather a library which has been
Ever since central to life of the mind
In erst "howling wilderness." I come in **

Bright afternoons amiably inclined
To reassure those founding magnates we
Yet bless their names for boons they left behind.

The southwest table shines eloquently
As I spread files along its tempered grain,
Whispering of the exalted company

I keep, so settled. Brightest of the chain,
DuBose wrote his best novel sitting here.
Who knows? Inspiration may strike again,

Bid me like *Peter Ashley* render clear
Veiled episodes of the proud past we share.
There are times he seems elbow-brushing near,

None more so than when I rise and repair
To the cloakroom where nothing has been changed
Save towels. A palpable presence there—

Tweed jacket, temporarily estranged,
Hook-hung as he ponders how best to save
A sickly sentence. Clauses rearranged,

We flush with one whoosh, proceeding to lave
At a Beaux Arts basin before reclaiming
Place and pens to resume the artist's brave

Battle with void white, the eternally shaming
Failure to pluck the choicest fruit that lurks
Just back of technique's reach, chimney the flaming

Vision. When I too have become my works,
Breathing, if at all, through successors' bellows,
What will live besides a few quips and quirks,

Ambered gossip? I'd gladly join my fellows,
Heyward, Paul Hayne, as a beneficent shade,
Content, while reputation's green leaf yellows,

To haunt the table where my songs were made,
Tending a pulse of continuity
For kin unborn assuming parts I played,
Awaiting wordless cloakroom colloquy.

---

* The seventeen gentlemen who founded the Charles Town Library Society in 1748 stated that they did so to lessen the danger of their descendants "sinking into savagery."
** Dr. Thomas Dale, congratulating Charlestonians on their rapid cultural advancement in a 1736 "Prologue" to *The Orphan*, reminded them that Carolina had been just that not long since.

Between the Rail and the Altar

I.P.M. The Revd. Canon S.T.C. *

Let us pray.

For forty years you said, and crooked your flock
  Through Cranmer to the altar where I served,
Many sires' son, and harkened, each time struck
  By that so humid drawl somehow preserved
From generations south, and thus waxed old
Shepherding bluebloods in a Wrenesque fold.

Your twilight's acolyte, watching you fail
  From the crisp credence, whence Sunday by same
I passed the elements, then at the rail
  Tipped chalice, bent after your shrinking frame,
That frayed mauve cassock's shower-curtain droop
Ballooning in the lustre of my cup.

You deftly razored most ingrained pretence.
  As I tugged a wrong-sized alb one early church,
Then ceased all effort with a frustrate flounce,
  You set us both right with a master-touch,
Soothing as you deflated, "Seabrook, you
Won't make Miss America, but you'll do."

You plucked my demons, and brought out my best—
  That time when, in the consecration-prayer
I rugby-dove to catch the raining Host
  Some hieratic swish launched unaware—
Forgot the marble steps until I landed
Agony-racked but happily fleet-handed.

And then, your swansong Easter in the chancel
   Proclaiming Christ the first-fruits of the dead,
Heart you had yet, but no longer the muscle
   To lift the filled King's Flagon, so I did;
The smile that kindled in your rheumy eyes
Repaid a thousand dawns' sleep-sacrifice.

Still when you went I did not weep at once,
   Or all that dank November week, until
The empty chancel crazed my equipoise,
   Then *sotto voce* sobbed as organ-swell
Surged to the close you taught is not our end,
Faithful soldier and servant, peerless friend.

* Samuel Thompson Cobb, born in Jacksonville on 14 May 1916, was rector and then rector emeritus of St. Philip's Church, Charleston from 1965 until his death there on 29 November 2003.

INTERLEAVED LUSTRE

The miff-maff-muff of water, the vocables
Of the wind, the glassily-sparkling particles
Of the mind.

  —Wallace Stevens, "Page from a Tale"

Drawing-room brimful with afternoon sun—
A pipe of white port. We turned to the wall
Void of windows, studied the chimney-breast
Where mirror-ranks of swaying nymphs processed
Towards a central sunburst; covering all
A roux of gloss, layers that one by one

Had fogged its features, smudged once-crisp detail
To shadowy blurs my eyes would see the same
Were it pristine. My hostess gestured where
Some blockhead elected to sand it clear,
Erasing two faces before he came
To his senses, got bored, or put up for sale

The house my friends are deeply conscious they
But hold in trust, hazarding I might know
Whose proper pains would unclog and refresh
Their most-prized mantel's too too solid flesh.
I could not help, and wondered, saying so,
Where else *faux* restoration breeds dismay,

How many of the thinning ranks of full-
Paneled Georgian chambers have been renewed
Beyond repair. Might in some revenant
Lodged between pea-princess blankets of paint
Wait distinctive shards of smalt, that elude
All eyes but most expert? Ah, to reveal

Time-tombed treasure fleck by patient fleck, then,
Faithful to lost methods, to recreate
The dizzy sensation of a room become
A wet watercolour while yet that room—
Blue washes' flickering swirls reanimate
Panels that dozed a dozen coats! And when,

Refracted from the harbour, sun slants up
To strike the glass-flakes sanding the surface,
The walls become a sparkling moonlit sea!
How much in lower life as art must be
Couched to dazzle! A single telltale trace—
If one but had a notion where to scrape.

PICTURE-GOERS AT AN EXHIBITION

Preview of Paintings by Horace Talmadge Day,
Gibbes Gallery, Charleston, 18 November 2004

Not a frightfully formal "do," but still
   A preponderance of *Madame-X* necks
(A few decidedly over the hill),
   Some canyoning the coruscating rocks
Or Scythian gold co-sponsors retail
(Pictures, unlike those baubles, not for sale).

Too many look as though accountants bade
   Them show and be seen, sniffing potential
Partners in ventures primed to put to shade
   Mere art's commercial clout—how pitiful
The strut of such lucre-spurred cocks, who crow
By business plan, and flame no combs to show!

And some there be who come to view yon daubs
   Not to display the cleavage God denied,
But knowledge *ditto*. No image disturbs
   Their self-regard, or backhands marble pride
For whom each canvas is but *point d'appui*
For riffs on their sublime complacency.

And then the pious remnant who blink tears
   Before Day's vistas, quaffing deep delight
In vernal sunshine laid down sixty years,
   Kissing the hand that caught precisely right
Light-quirks our local eyes have always known,
Lending us back what we presumed our own.

A quasi-Masonic complicity
   Entwines the glad band who alike revere
The artist and the landscapes that set free
   His brush to soar so: We, met briefly here,
Pilgrims for whom this cramped space shines a shrine,
Gaze drunk on beauty as with salvered wine.

TED

I.P.M. Ted Ashton Phillips, Jr.
(1 November 1959–17 January 2005)

Almost as much a fixture in our midst
As the spire in whose long shadow you lived,
Whence leaden-hearted we took you to rest
At Magnolia, whose mysteries you delved,
Your twin pillars devotion and knowledge,
For every fact you found was bathed in love.
Your learning was never distinction's badge—
You had no grudge to grind, no worth to prove.

You were the genius of our storied place.
As I recall our doorstep colloquies
I cannot contemplate that empty space,
You shrunk to a welter of memories.
Translated, rather—for how could you cease
Marrying true minds, putting wrong things right?
You are busy, friend, in body's new peace
Enhancing the lives of angels of light.

ALMOST AUTUMNAL

Surviving the Charleston summer once more
  Merits a medal, save such would reflect
    The shrunk-from sun, sear decorated breast
  Like branding guilt: knowing what to expect
    Aids not a whit, one is no less hard-pressed,
Fights no fiercer for having lost before.

It's been another protracted campaign,
  To which each year one drags less heart, forsooth—
    We suffer most, we of the mezzanine stage
  Between the insouciant resilience of youth
    And past-caring impotence of old age,
Our ebbing strength unequal to the strain.

No charm to ward white noon's ox-felling blow;
  Like stepping out of a capsule on Mars,
    Mere walking cops an insanity plea,
  Even twilights lingered in well-chilled bars
    Sugar not signs of deep malignity
In lives we less enjoy than undergo.

But lo, this morn, untrumpeted, praise be!
  The crested heat recedes, that miracle
    Each endless summer melts all memory of:
  A shyly smiling sun shines peaceable,
    A sprightly breeze makes it delight to move
About outside, not grim necessity.

So unaccustomed not to sag oppressed
  By air alone, under sustained attack
    From foes exhaustless, suddenly I see
  The whole disposition seem to tilt back
    To some occluded equanimity;
The world feels kinder than one would have guessed.

SPIDER-LILIES

Gorgeous transients, they always surprise
Our summer-sated eyes
In mid-September.

We feast on these marvels a few charmed days
Then go our wintry ways
And misremember

Them quite by next autumnal equinox,
So that their scarlet shocks
Our startled senses

As ambling our usual churchyard walks
We spy their naked stalks'
Calyx-crowned fences

Tracing ancestral plots, or squadron-massed
Round headstones we brush past
Most days without thought.

Like the pious dead from whose mold they rise
These lilies briefly blaze,
Then shrivel to naught;

In death's long pause one could do worse than feed
Such coronals, which need
Nor leaves nor stages

To perfect their act, and never outstay
Wonder, hasting away
Like bonfire pages.

The Last of October

Cloudbank-clearing light with successive shocks
Ignites a sycamore, beaten-gold slant
Transforming dun-green of departing leaves
To the satisfied glow of gathered sheaves;
I widen eyes while students observant
As Bartimaeus slouch to eight o'clocks.

Mind paints the land departing glaciers built
Where my friend Charles charts with acutest eye
And expert pen more dramatic divesting
Of summer's boast. This month, with colour cresting,
I too might witness ranges multiply
Yon urban giant whose treasure's unspilt,

But mountain-top experience were now
Too far beyond what latter days require;
A solitary tree sufficiently speaks
As life contracts with myriad timber-creaks,
A local charm the utmost I desire—
Beauty of one late bloom, warmth of one brow.

A MARTINMAS BUTTERFLY

> I cannot rest from travel: I will drink
> Life to the lees.
>
> —Tennyson, "Ulysses," ll. 6–7

Taking this lease for the bounty it is,
Through summer's coda you tack your soundless
Way with what looks the fastidiousness
Of a dilettante—rather Ulysses,
For you quaff your briefer burst to the lees,
Each fresh day dawning, as for me it is,

Sheer miracle, jewel of this one you
Settling on a miniature-zinnia clump
Leaded-glass wings you continue to pump,
Its blooms' brash orange toned down half a tint,
Naught owing harmony or taken hint,
For instinct arrows August's residue.

Nuance and shifting tones fret such as I;
The one right target gained, you dip to work
Oblivious what death or dangers lurk—
Tonight Canadian cold may barrel down,
Muddy lingering brilliance to null brown.
Your hinges dimple as you drain life dry.

NOVEMBER CYPRESSES

I notched their charms all our serpentine way
To Wilmington and back, golden flambeaux
Clumped in select cul-de-sacs amid grey
Of lesser-breed trunks, sure I did not know
How brush might corner such elusive tones,
Convinced my circumspect washes would fail
To simulate simmer, even Allston's
Venetian broth of glazes, his vermeil
Danaë-shower of Titianesque technique,
Might shy of muster. Later in the week

Lapping the luxury of standing still
I eye an urban cousin at close range
Parsing the hybrid-colour strands until
Juice of seized meaning jets light on the strange
Attraction in this half-way house between
Stevensian "total grandeur" of poured gold *
And spring's first implausibly tender green.
Cusp trembles: to plunge into bronze, or hold
Fast breathing tree till fabric fall apart—
Eternal hide-and-seek of Life and Art.

* The penultimate stanza of Wallace Stevens's poem for his old Harvard professor
George Santayana, "To An Old Philosopher in Rome":

It is a kind of total grandeur at the end,
With every visible thing enlarged and yet
No more than a bed, a chair and moving nuns,
The immense theatre, the pillared porch,
The book and candle in your ambered room.

Three strands of Virginia creeper, scarlet
  In their own right and the rising sun's rays,
    Snake paired glazed leaves across the sullen red
  Brick upper back of a warehouse—spare craze
    Of vestigial coils roping a bald head,
Or, leapt from a scene no one could forget

In Price's Eutaw tale, lash-souvenirs,
  Risen welts ridged where ribbon flesh was rent,
    Whose scars will accuse when the scarlet fades.
  Or rather hymn such laudable intent,
    To reach beyond themselves ere cold invades
And their strength falters with the fading year's:

Arrow-aspiring, hostage nor to whims
  Nor doubts, nor falling back on self, sublime
    Simplicity of aim, to colonize,
  Latching successors' support as they climb
    To end in a blaze that dazzles all eyes
Until death's leaden grip snaps their spent stems.

URBAN CRIME

I. GERIATRIC DELINQUENCY

The world a fever-blur as I creep west
  Towards sickbed with fetched food I fancy not,
Sunk to a bench for modicum of rest,
  I turn to taste the journey's one bright spot,

The sprightly arcs and startling buttercup
  Of a *Cassia* at height across the street.
A well-dressed blue-rinse beldam fetches up,
  Face tilted, rapture by the look complete.

Recognizing a kinship of gladdened eye
  (Awareness of beauty met seldom enough),
I rise to share her joy, draw smiling nigh
  As she snaps the best bloom-cluster clean off

And beats retreat, unspeakable old hag,
  Clutching it to deathwatch dugs! I recoil
As though an asp leapt from my shopping-bag,
  And, fevered two ways now, commence to boil.

Had she no faintest notion this display
  Might be for public benefit? Alas,
Shall branch spun to brighten passers' drear day
  Snuff in spent trollop's Carnival-glass vase?

All faults we execrate in befogged young—
  Selfishness that cannot properly be,
Given social autism, too unstrung
  To comprehend sense of community

With other people, who no more exist
  Than wonders of the past—now to find these
Foul elders not so readily dismissed
  As ignorant...! Was this crone schooled to please

34

Self merely by a mother who saw light
   Before the earthquake? Ah, it shakes again, *
Certainties shiver in encircling night.
   What shrunk-patch shreds of decency remain?

Shall we airbrush crude theft with psychobabble?
   Is any help to hand? I am unable.
Civility is dead—bring on the rabble.
   May the vase tip and stain your shining table.

* In Charleston, time is still to some extent measured with reference to the great
earthquake of 31 August 1886.

II. GRAND THEFT

Dwarfed by White's magnificent hexastyle,
   Most correct Doric in our templed city,
A shrunken Holy Family raise a smile,
   Looking less objects of reverence than pity.

Not a full house, as manger groupings go—
   Holies, two shepherds, some sad sheep betwixt.
Perhaps these high-toned A.M.E.'s are so
   Orthodox their Wise Men wait till the sixth?

Such as it is, the gathering's old-school white:
   No hint of Coppertone or compromise.
It is as though they still view Christmas night
   Through the original congregation's eyes. *

I reflect, with nothing more urgent to do,
   As shoppers run Mammon's gauntlet on King,
This crèche echoes the Christmas childhood knew
   Ere plastic charged and coated everything.

They've set the same scuffed scene out fifty years
　　Without one makeover or touch-up brush,
Aware the point is not how it appears,
　　But whether it helps hearts kneel in awed hush.

Strolling towards sunset Christmas afternoon
　　I pause as heretofore, but sense, perplexed,
Something amiss—and editing eyes soon
　　Expose the solecism in their text.

Jesus is gone! Crib cradles emptiness,
　　Only frond-strips absorb adoring eyes!
Mine dart about in extrovert distress,
　　But He is truly gone—they tell no lies.

Slick perp must have sloped up the handicap
　　Where the grille's been removed. Even police
Can piece the how, but *why*? What way to map
　　A mind that would purloin the Prince of Peace?

What street credit might a fifty-year-old
　　Out-of-shape snow-crab white baby command?
The trail of motive straightway runs corpse-cold.
　　Would even no-show Wise Men understand?

What vile mutation of cupidity,
　　Snatching Jesus as though He were a purse?
The hope of all the world pawned for a high?
　　Mind cannot fathom, or would wish to, worse.

This unimaginably wicked deed
　　Speaks sickness earthly agents cannot heal.
O come to us! Each hour more sore our need
　　Of the Christ-Child promise no thief can steal.

---

* Designed by the astonishingly versatile Edward Brickell White, the church at 60 Wentworth Street, Charleston, was constructed in 1841–42 for the white congregation of Second Baptist Church. After it merged with another white Baptist congregation at the war's end, the building was purchased in 1866 by a group of black congregants who had declined Trinity Methodist's offer to make them members provided they continue to sit in the gallery. The congregation of Centenary Methodist Church have owned and cared for White's architectural masterpiece ever since.

WORDSWORTH IN HARLESTON VILLAGE

"There was a roaring in the wind all night;" *
Yestere'en your rhyme chimed with local fact.
You might have felt at home, quaffing delight
In sounds like those of cliff-launched cataract,
Save when the roar would suddenly contract
To anxious huffing too leaky to wreak
Destruction on a Titan's house-high name-day cake.

Most days you'd not have cozied to this clime.
Prospect of American settlement
Fanned Coleridge's fancy for a time;
Not yours—boyhood foreknew age need be spent
Among those mighty cradling forms that lent
Majesty to utterance from the first;
Our Lowcountry could not have slaked your mountain thirst.

A laureate of English seasons' change
Would fret in pulsing fever of amaze—
Bulbs before Christmas? Strange—and yet more strange,
Ice swiftly dissolving in barefoot days!
You'd have been as perplexed at our shore's ways
As this non-winter azaleas have been:
Before flowering is quite finished, they bud again.

Reliable goad of vein-piercing damp
Nourished your spirit, but no more shall I
Shiver vigil for spring's fickle-wicked lamp
In your land, where many a westward sigh
Hissed vernal expectations gone awry,
The teaser tantalizing into May
Without sop-satisfaction of one shirtsleeve day.

I purpose to remove my creaking bones
To an isle where seasons scarcely pertain,
Where no chafing of sleet and raw wind hones
Hardihood to sculpt melody of pain,
But trades riffle fronds, gusts rarely complain,
April's a joy remembered, sun-blanched hint
Of floribundant present prodigal of scent

And colour beyond northern eye's chapped ken,
Hibiscus, heliconia, orchid tree.
I rally to begin the world again,
Perhaps to issue shoots in sympathy,
Warm-bath calm soothing and inspiring me
As gales blessed your flame, trebly blessed to come,
Now shadows mass, on a place heart pronounces home.

---

* The opening line of Wordsworth's "Resolution and Independence" (1802; published 1807); I appropriate his stanza form as well. Harleston Village, laid out as a garden suburb, has long since been absorbed by her rhyme-partner Charleston, but remains conspicuously leafy. Born from a house in Harleston, I have lived there intermittently ever since.

GRAY'S ORCHID-TREE

One morn I miss'd him on the custom'd hill,
Along the heath and near his fav'rite tree.
—"Elegy Written in a Country Church Yard," ll. 109–10

One morn I sense some landmark is not there,
    Pausing as usual to tick inventory
(Good exercise to keep eyes in repair).
    Spot sequestered in tousled canopy
White knots uncurling tongues in debonair
    Bon mots—ach, flown the blossom and the tree!
Hope peers around banked vine, but no mistake:
Not one shed bivalve leaf is left to rake.

What odds it was not spirited away,
    But never *was* there, mere mirage, eye-tease
Planting siren flora to haste the day
    Of departure I hesitate to seize?
The parallel lines I repeat from Gray
    Fetch no crumb-comfort, rather stoke unease,
Confirming when life waxes most perplexed
I tend to turn to, or create, a text.

Too symptomatic, then, not to be real—
    To have been, for at curfew-toll I find
Quotidian comforts without warning steal
    Away, steal ... sad stumps ruefully remind
Of all that once—whine not, but how conceal
    The bitterness of fruit gnawed to the rind?
What disappears is never hurt or pain,
But boons one would stake heart's blood to retain.

Always the likes of you, white orchid-tree!
    Was it wise to uproot? Can you withstand
So huge a shock, and relocated be
    Happier, flourish afresh in new-found land?
You were text all along, I come to see:
    The selfsame questions punctuate my planned
Last-ditch fall back to where the country ends
To give life one last chance to make amends.

39

SORCERESS CITY

I.

As though she read and rued settling intent
    On return from her rival to pronounce
Our trial separation permanent,
    Old Charleston assumes such a countenance
As would make sterner will than mine relent—
    Ranging a lifetime's first-light strolls, not once
Can memory approach this nonpareil dawn
For which she draws all her witcheries on.

II.

I latch the garden gate in thinning dark
    And zigzag silent streets to set face east,
Threading undulant shade of drowsing park
    To High Battery, goal of my modest quest,
Expecting the usual expanse—but hark,
    Instead front an Adam-mantel sunburst,
Chiseled cloud-slits through which the trapped gold slips,
Spoked symmetries of a perfect ellipse.

III.

Each remove wafts fresh the whelming perfume
    Of Confederate Jasmine, haunting like
Aesthetic conscience, as bloom by charged bloom
    I ply quotidian tasks, pausing to drink
Nectar from gilt gesso swags, then resume
    More languid for my sea-girt's well-shaped work,
Decking herself for Venetian espousal *
With every trick of sensual arousal.

IV.

And then the *coup de grâce* with eve's descent—
    I lounge in oak-recess as zephyrs stir
Simmers of birdsong and ripe-orange glint,
    Shadowing vast branches aloft to where
Crescent moon hangs a bright-cut ornament
    Between ferned gestures and the folding star. **
Challenge sounds clear as far light, "Do you dare
Bid lasting farewell to a queen so fair?"

* Perhaps the grandest of the Venetian pageants was the *Sensa*, the celebration of the wedding of the Venetian Republic and the Adriatic, observed annually on Ascension Day from 1100. Accompanied by an immense retinue, the Doge was rowed in his state barge, the *Bucintoro*, to the Lido, where he cast a gold ring into the water and declared, "We espouse thee, O Sea, in token of our true and perpetual dominion over thee." Charleston has long fancied herself an analogue of Venice, and has of course enjoyed her own, rather briefer, interludes as a proudly independent republic. This poem is set at Ascensiontide.
** The "folding star" is the evening star, which appears as shepherds drive their charges to the fold. In *Comus* Milton evokes "The star that bids the shepherds fold" (l. 93), and William Collins' "Ode to Evening" includes this atmospheric touch: "When thy folding- star arising shows/His paly circlet" (l. 72). *The Folding Star* is also the title of Alan Hollinghurst's whelmingly beautiful 1994 novel of debilitating desire.

ELECTRIC LIGHT, A SCREENED PORCH AND A HUNDRED CHICKENS

CLARENDON COUNTY, SOUTH CAROLINA—1943

Night after night he rocks on the screened porch,
Glaring into the dark. Like other folks
Decades together, they're locked tongue and groove
And have their rituals. Dora will come and say,
"Hon, yo' settin' in de dahk," and switch on
The overhead light, and Edwin will snap,
"Shut dat dam' t'ing off—wha' Ah wan' tuh *see*?"
Then she'll laugh and pad on back to the kitchen,
Her new stove that hums like those giant turbines
Down at Santee Dam—not that he's been there *
Or has mind to go, but it's hard to ignore
Papers stuffed with the project's miracles.
He wonders what she's cooking for all the time:
Just so much fat you can pile on one spine,
And they were big already—ain't no need
With the children long scattered. She reckon
She can ship coconut cakes to the troops,
Like she some production-line for the war?
He snorts. Women got no sense of the world.
This whole mess she read like a comic-strip,
Act like she won a raffle when they cut the check,
Blind to the loss column. Squawking out yon!
Three-four hens stuck in bad dreams. Do they dream?
He does, but only nightmares since the move—
Seized up like Lot's wife and drowned, house and all.
Old sweet sleep gone, hearing through its soft folds
Tree-frogs and big bass bulls shake the swamp's heart.
Dam' chickens! If they ain't at it again!
He hopes they don't all rouse like night 'fore last—
Woke them round two. A fox, he sighed, but doubts:
No point prowling this sorry-ass scrub-pine:
No cover to speak of—sho' wish a fox
Would come and tear their rumps to rags. The eggs!

What they 'spose do with so many? He groans,
"Fixin' tuhn *inter* a egg!" And she drawls,
Lobbing him her sauciest bedroom look,
"Yo' 'bout dat shape aw'reddy." He *has*
Put on, he knows, now there's no land to work,
And didn't put in a garden this spring.
He doesn't trust red clay; besides, the fools
Paid so much for the farm he can afford **
To rock and remember—always circling back
To the same spot, loved best from barefoot boy,
That oldest stand of virgin cypress left,
Their trunks so huge the whole family
Couldn't join hands round one: When each child came
They'd try again—another ritual.
And the light in that grove, where ancient trees
Seemed to stretch high as God, and sunrays fell
Through clotted green mist of millions of needles
To snuff their candles in the water's pitch.
He's started to notice how his memories
Get more mixed up each time he unwraps one,
Warping, distorting, the straight lines swole up
Like the whole past was under water too.

---

* Most of the 901 families displaced in 1939–41 to make way for the Santee Cooper hydroelectric scheme were poor black farmers. Where possible, their houses were moved; otherwise new houses were constructed for them by the Authority. Each dwelling was equipped with electricity, and windows and porches were given screens, then still a rarity in the rural South. Each family was also presented with a bonus of one hundred chickens. The poem's title is that of my lead article on the earlier history of Santee Cooper in the *Charleston Mercury* of 18 August 2005.
** The displaced landowners were given $12.19 an acre when the going rate for agricultural land in South Carolina was about two dollars an acre.

II. Consanguinity

Where'er on earth the self-devoted heart
Hath been by worthy deeds exalted thus,
We look for proud exemplars; yet for us
    It is enough to know
Our fathers left us freemen; let us show
The will to hold our lofty heritage,
The patient strength to act our fathers' part.

—Paul Hamilton Hayne, "My Mother-Land"

PIAZZA PEACE

My darkling piazza's hushed peace succumbs
  To the clop of mounted-police patrol;
Recessive rhythm of flintlock hooves thrums
  Like the bass of a spectral barcarolle.

As stillness reigns again I clasp the rail
  Craning west to the house a block along
Where parents, newly married, trimmed blithe sail
  For lifelong voyage that would soon tack wrong,

And wonder whether like song reached their ears
  As they, foreknowing me, sat sipping night
That other mild October all those years
  Before their heir saw and squandered the light.

CEDARS

From afar, simple of shape as in mood.
  Apparent groves are herds of soloists
  For whom nearest neighbour scarcely exists,
Blessed or cursed with inherent solitude.

The assorted offspring that encompass
  A mournful matriarch remain discreet,
  Splendid in self-possession as complete
As stepping-stone issue on a knight's brass.

Yet awesomely complex viewed from within—
  I look up the robe of a patriarch
  To cloudless cobalt veining layered dark.
Detail enough to exhaust most patient pen:

Beyond depiction those immensities
  Of angled spokes that meld to shade my seat.
  A flake of fragrance, loosened by the heat,
Floats my way on an absent-minded breeze.

Mind's eye settles on Mother's cedar-chest,
  Where she kept, balmed and shrined like true relic,
  Father's letters home from the Pacific—
Of all her worldly goods the ones loved best.

Bundles I've never felt worthy to untie—
  The air-mailed love of a wartime vestal
  Keeping body pure till it prove mortal
Or he returned to obviate reply.

Truer love in his longing phrased in the vein
  Of band-songs to which Mother shadow-waltzed,
  Than in the mode this off-base age exalts,
With naught to veil or defer or restrain.

For lining the drawers designed to contain
  What we most wish to keep, cedar is best.
  His mawkish late-teen words can have expressed
Little of heart's depths, less the exquisite pain,

Never perhaps to know what he had missed;
  But words were not what he was careful of—
  It was the self preserved for his one love.
He smelt of cedar when at last they kissed.

A FEW GOOD PIECES

As box by box, piece by good piece they rouse
From dusty sleep delights long stashed away,
Far-scattered props of bruised gentility,
The interlude languished is, it strikes me,
Fairy-tale deferral's year and a day—
But sans the won princess to grace new house.

Already, as its naked boards echoed
Methought it might evoke parents' first nests
When at war's end their leaden waiting bloomed.
Now furnishing begins, another tombed
Life reassembles, as this space suggests
My furthest-remembered childhood abode.

Set apart, the Philadelphia chair
Looks pleased with its progress, and well it might,
Smiling as value steadily increases.
Our sparse array of choice family pieces
Shrinks from the sharp appraisal of hindsight,
Those walls and hardwoods Cinderella-bare.

Once ferreted out of their hiding-places,
My gems will coruscate—fat years brought back
Something of the tone of the world we lost
In Sixty-Five. What grandsires' conflict cost
Troubled them not, nor looted treasures' lack,
For they had love to bridge their empty spaces.

We navigate our spans as we elect:
With love so plain even a child might see
They chose each other; I select Chinese,
Bubbled, crated, awaiting surfaces—
English oak, black walnut, mahogany—
That will display their glories to effect.

Why is it as I pick my path downhill
(Tendency grown too settled to disguise)
I seem to shadow progenitors' lives?
This heart on guilty retrospection thrives—
All horribly awry, I realize,
As though scales fell: however high I fill,

Where pitch Chinese-Chippendale pleasure-dome,
It will ring hollow, for false impulse drove
(Tracing tendrils of a Rococo scroll)
Acquisition—beauty squeezed dry my soul,
While, wiser and dead, they anchored in love,
That serves alone to build and fill a home.

SARAH

A loved grandmother's name, and hers, and high
Up the entangled branches of our tree—
Lovely sound, but tell me not euphony
Alone led many mothers to confer
Those sigh-pouch syllables on a daughter;
I trust some naming dames heard not the sigh

But lofty promise, wished the christened child
In twilit life unlooked-for happiness.
Having revered out great progenitress
My many days, astonished now I feel
Her rapt joy not in scripture but my real
And present rapture as dead-letter filed

Ambitions blaze like massed Michaelmas daisies:
My chance to flare a Chatterton long past,
Pent songs of youth flood full-spate, born at last.
I too would have been hasty to deride
Last winter, had some angel prophesied
That ere chill came again I should amaze

Myself and friends by authoring more verse
Than in the previous score of fallow years:
Midlife's cloistral calm stacks the bright arrears
Of laurels impetuous youth thought to pluck
For the asking; dizzied by lightning luck,
Enchanted knight awaking from a curse,

Grateful and groggy, slow to understand
How gifts for which one had forgot to yearn
Arrive unasked, grace too precious to earn,
Green growth where barrenness blighted so long,
Sepulchral womb alive with sudden song
As quite despaired-of hopes quicken to hand.

THE CHILDREN'S HOUR

"Each age is a dream that is dying
or one that is coming to birth."
—Franklin D. Roosevelt, as quoted by George W. Bush

I can picture both, that I used to muddle
With Grandfather, connecting by some queer
Associative pole-vault his marble pate
With the mottled polish of their veneer.
Silent both, as Gran Joseph soon would be,
Demoted to furniture. His still sat
Emparloured in patronal armchair's lee.
Grandsire John had banished his grander model

To the gloom of a garret passage-way
Where my face met its stretched-cloth fish-mouth gape
Each morning as I turned to skip downstairs
To breakfast cherishing new-risen hope
That this bright day Father had woken stronger.
We made friends, lips wet the cloth with my fears
Till Mother's tears told he would writhe no longer,
Like my friend have nothing further to say.

Listening last night to the State of the Union
On my healthy ghetto with lights-out sips,
Resting eyes after long day's rhyme-safari,
I summoned maternals with smile-wreathed lips
Flanking like firedogs the crackling machine,
Spellbound by Mr. Roosevelt's uncanny
Gift for reassurance as he made plain
A war-rent world's intractable confusion,

Gran Sarah's hair a lamp-globe blanched with flame.
Dark as it grew, how simple their world seems,
With identifiable enemies,
Shared values, hopes and fears and postwar dreams!
I flared with envy long assumed outgrown,
Not for such comfortable certainties
But of idealist Joseph, decades gone,
Whose President, his friend, called him by name—

Not the connexion, but his perfect faith
In the man, such as I have never kept
For an official, even the one speaking
For whom I voted, whose victory whooped.
As I woke from a third brief nap, the incumbent
Closed his speech with Roosevelt's words—heart-shaking
Coincidence that seemed that instant sent
To scythe through all my tare-strewn years, and bathe

This thwarted body in a healing stream,
The haven of laps into which I'd climb,
Fall fast asleep soothed by their tender touch,
Sarah's and Joseph's, who kept me the time
Surgeons first cut—of all the world unsure
Save they were good, and loved me very much.
Small, frail, innocent, utterly secure:
As presidents pitch, "Each age is a dream."

A WITHERED ARM

I.P.M. Professor Francis Welborn

Great-great grandsire on the Maryland side,
Born with planter blood but a withered arm,
    And thus unfit to farm,
Was sent to school and college to equip
    Him for professorship.
Greek he loved, grasped verb by torturous verb—
His hunger for knowledge nothing could curb
Till oysterwise the Attic world valved wide.

He doled out its riches for sixty years,
Pulsing light young charges could not resist.
    Lately, through no twist
Of nature, but olympic clumsiness,
    Stumbling I chanced to press
Some spring in my right arm that made it seize,
Balk unbending. Through vexed indignities
Of left-hand eating, dressing, throbbed forked fears

This freak suspension might prove permanent,
Snap my able-bodied span to dead halt
    With atavistic vault
To great Greek grandsire's frozen inflection.
    Essaying to poke fun
At distaff heroics of knife and spoon
But raising hollow chuckles, I was soon
Transfixed before a worse impediment.

Failing to find the mouth at first attempt—
Grotesque indeed, but in the wider scheme
    Miles from direst extreme,
Which must be when sovereign mind can no more
    Augment its golden store,
Then finds, at first suspecting hands unseen,
Memory's larder each raid becomes more lean,
At length accepting itself not exempt

From winding-down of flesh. Were I to find
I could no more from Heliconian springs
      Cup fresh imaginings,
Or grasp loved masters' or my own hands' song,
      Grant I might not prolong
Slack days beyond my talents' pilgrimage,
Sorrow mere being would no wise assuage.
Let me not outlast the life of the mind.

UNCLAIMED TREASURES

Full many a gem of purest ray serene,
The dark unfathom'd caves of ocean bear:
Full many a flower is born to blush unseen,
And waste its sweetness on the desert air.

—Thomas Gray, "Elegy Written in a Country Church Yard," ll. 53-56

Easier far for flora to blush unseen—
Next door's solo bush sports one perfect pink
West-facing jewel wooing my eyes alone.
It seems not to mind being on its own,
Adept as partnered peers at beauty's blink,
One day a star, then brown-bordered has-been.

Flowers put forth perforce—that is how they live,
Expecting no commerce, deaf to the snap
Of stem when they are singled to swim
In epergne, smile on heaped sideboard at whim
Of hostess. For them there is no skewed hap:
They simply spread the pleasure theirs to give.

But those who spread the other sideboard treats,
Maiden aunts Mother bade us never call
With wag-tongues "unclaimed treasures"—poor old dears,
Preserves on pantry-shelves, desiccate years
Trailing after florescence met a wall,
Blank indifference that left untouched their sweets.

Aunt Katharine told Mother she'd ached to wed,
But the right man never happened her way.
Not hers to unfurl symmetrical bud
As camellia come to its zenith would,
Programmed to perfect predestined display
Whether or no it turned admirer's head.

Wormwood to have a wealth of love to share
And find no takers, presenting brave face
Fading in step with hope the dreamt right one
Might dawn at last, with nothing to be done
Save practice useful arts, cultivate grace,
And put off that sour-eyed suitor despair.

The ranks of unclaimed blossoms on our tree
Haunt me this winter's dusk, who share their doom,
Thus late it dawns, and, pray, their fortitude.
Compounding trenched chill, rising wind with rude
Fingers shakes last light from my private bloom.
The single state we share was meant to be.

POSES

I.P.M. Robert T. S. Lowell

A ghost-click frames my stance with camera's eye:
Relaxing downwards from this stoop-top seat
I ape a famous snapshot of young you,
Elbows on wide-splayed knees they jab into
As tip-touched hands and collarbone complete
A hexagon that locks in place ... my sigh.

This overstuffed torso's no longer taut,
And draped, for which relief much thanks, yet still
Somehow that camp vignette, summer before
Harvard, a counselor already sure
You would be a poet, already full
Of the hurt that stutters through all you wrote.

I was certain of nothing; my prelude
Begun in Rome closed at the Albert Hall
With Barbirolli's last symphonic Mahler.
Goose-gorged on Jamesian repast, scant wonder
I found Cambridge disappointingly small
And Freshman English not my kind of food.

With *Alma* we both quarreled and made peace.
You were at war with the State when we met,
Your face as far as my grisaille now is
From seventeenth summer, but kind lens froze
An off-duty counselor whose white-hot
Genius would melt critics to mercy-pleas.

If a lens periscoped behind that fence
What would it record? Hand-fast arms embrace
Left knee while right leg dangles unhinged sides
Of outsize polygon: What message rides
On the shift? Does candid straight-ahead face
Sieve through artfully-posed insouciance

What long day's Crow-shadow has not erased:
This morn I was stung to a depth long thought
Beyond the range of a cooling heart's feeling,
Slapped down in the chancel by the befouling
Tongue of sheepskin-cloaked friend, unkindest cut
That sprung a fountain of hurt-laced disgust.

Dear moldering Cuz, why do we live so long,
When each day's lesson is forbear to trust,
And that unlearnt? Your smiling open pose—
Better, alas, crouched tense against fresh blows!
Too old my heart to ward betrayal's thrust;
I weary of pretending to be strong.

Sole answer found, the Crow I loft's unclear,
Frosted like nightmare tarn I ache to reach,
And plunge the latest wound for cold to lick;
My few high dives in Cedar Mountain's lake, *
When toes touched bottom, sprang from squidgy thatch,
I wondered had I breath to rise to air.

* Cedar Mountain, straddling the border between North and South Carolina, is the location of Camp Greenville, where for more than a dozen summers, as camper and then counselor, the poet swam in frigid Lake Rotary.

The Genealogist's Lament

I shrink abashed! Abetting monstrous pride,
Stoking ravenous egos of the rich—
My unmeant crimes rise up and call me fraud.
Lately I shaped a more consummate bitch
Of one pronounced before. What profits this?
My modest fees aside, who's aggrandized
By these proceedings, save to gain access
To some cabal of hooch-anaesthetized
Self-adulatory scion-sots who
Have leeched or pissed all virtues that propelled
Ancestors to found and sign and see through
Schemes of surpassing worth? Though quite unwilled
I have drawn out the worst in clients—and yet
In some few best, the latest chief among,
Her zeal for no vicarious coronet
But untrimmed truth. For such it is not wrong
To comb dim trees for answers, to explore
Jet recesses to tease the past to light,
For they rejoice on quite another shore
From Dames and Sons; their study founts delight,
Wondrous extension of allotted time,
Place, circle, family—from their raised dead
They gain associates, mentors, friends, they climb
Free of the foreground, schooled to see ahead
Better for peering backwards. Yes, they choose,
As one portions the living, and for me
This late mild autumn glowing as it goes,
Recalling in reverse the intensity
Of this season's tints in that distant land
Of schooling and the sternest of my blood,
My choice companions now, one on each hand,
New-England sires whose disparate talents flood
A shared conduit, Great-great Grandmother Jane.
What types of noble effort they afford!
Younger-son blacksmith's boy Nathanael Greene, *

61

Who beat his Quaker ploughshare back to sword
And forged a nation; then, further removed,
Apostle John Eliot, who laboured long **
To train Christ's light on the red men he loved,
Gentle, long-suffering, gloriously wrong—
His Wampanoag Bible a monument ***
To self-defeating scholarship, since they
Could no more read their tongue than his: well-meant,
But wide!—a circumstance ripe to convey
In its fundamental detachment of
Message from object his kinship to
Old-Testament prophet pouring tough love
On deaf ears, or his dozen-greats nephew
Who pens verses altogether less rough
Than his in *Bay Psalm Book*, but which also ****
Design to promote amendment of life.
A century apart both came to know
The paradox of sore-achieved defeat
Turning like autumn leaves to victory,
Crowns in history and heaven. Shall I repeat
Their pattern? For all I shan't, we shall see.

* General Nathanael Greene (1742–1786), a Rhode Island iron-founder until 1775; his brilliant conduct of the campaign in the South from 1780 denied the British any chance of claiming South Carolina and Georgia in the peace negotiations at war's end.

** The Reverend John Eliot (1604–1690). Cambridge-educated, he came to Massachusetts Bay in 1631 and ministered there for the next six decades. He was known as the "Apostle to the Indians," whom he proselytized from 1646 until his death.

*** His translation of the New Testament appeared in 1661; the Old Testament followed in 1663. This was the first Bible to be published in North America.

**** The *Bay Psalm Book*, the name commonly given to *The whole Booke of Psalmes, faithfully translated into English metre*. Published at Cambridge in 1640, this was the first American book. Most of the translations were made by John Eliot, Richard Mather, and Thomas Weld.

CAPTAIN CHRISTOPHER

(Christmas Night 2004)

Warm in the new house, warmer by the glass,
Surrounded by acres ours since time was *
In this parish, we take turn of year stock,
The black panes ghosting our mirrored selves back
As we shelve the spent leaf and peer ahead—
Cautiously, all save our host, who sprouts plans
And projections past tally for these lands
He bought back and now nurses from the dead:
Greenhouse framed, the new double avenue
To be set out come spring, varieties
Of vegetables multiplied, even bees
Dwarf my hopes of seeing this bottle through.

Suddenly I seize how it all began—
Fleet Street tavern, turn of William's eighth year,
Kit Wilkinson, kinsman's presumptive heir **
Still vaguely longing to be his own man
Clinks a bumper with two not long returned
From fabulous Carolina, who having duly wived
Take ship next week. Friend Maybank here has lived,
Not waited fawning—all for which he's yearned
Blooms in these magi-tales of lands afar!
At length resolved to share their southern star,
Raptly he foresees what may come to pass,
Warm in the "Olde Cock," warmer by the glass.

---

* Some of the lands on the Toogoodoo River in St. Paul's Parish granted to Governor
Landgrave Joseph Morton in 1682 have remained in possession of descendants of his
granddaughter the Lady Elizabeth, who married Captain Christopher Wilkinson
by contract of 1 December 1701.
** When he came out to Carolina about 1697, Christopher Wilkinson was heir-
presumptive to the Yorkshire estates of his cousin Francis Wilkinson of Lincoln's
Inn, Q.C. The old boy did not oblige his heir by expiring until 1728.

AUNT KATHARINE

In real life, if such exist, she was
  Only a distant cousin whose one brother
    Wed what sticklers in kin would certify
  That category, a sister to my mother:
    A classic maiden schoolmarm she, and I
A something in the making, her chief cause.

Each summer afforded a Proserpine
  Transom of opportunity, a lean
    Sea-island wedge to drive in shaping me
  Into the young man her son would have been—
    Island-bred boy, a consummate Geechee— *
Who languished in school above the fall-line.

How she bestirred her slacks, remodeled, delved,
  Chopped, simplified, fanned by fanatic zeal
    To cast me a *Good Ole* understudy
  Snug in the contours of her *Beau Ideal*,
    Fit for his place (at length piazza-worthy)
On ancestral isles where he'd scarcely lived.

I must have vexed her mightily when young;
  My talk she endured in minuscule doses—
    Thrall to soaring vocabulary inflation,
  Arcane, grandiose, a sunburst of lost causes
    Quite out of scale with our Post-Bellum station
And the homespun souls I would live among.

Deep-stung, I shrank, too sensitive to see
  Her wit-barbs riddled my pretentiousness
    Not for sick fun but to thicken my hide,
  Long-haul strength outweighing ten-tear distress,
    Her method's pudding-proof in my smooth glide
To repossession at majority.

64

Once from John's Island we moved up to Town
  Visiting cousins recumbent and quick,
    Were heading down Spring to the then one bridge
   As I high-hymned, trowelling three tropes thick,
    The heavenly joys of being a Rutledge,
When with a warning sniff she shot me down.

"So what?" she snapped. We cleared respective throats.
  "See those darkeys on every door-stoop yon?
    My high-toned scion, I have news for you!
   Whole piazzas full—get a good look, son.
    Guess what? Half of them are Rutledges too;
Here's where your Signers stashed their ill-sown oats." **

Back home that same summer she deputized
  A golden Pinckney cousin years my elder,
    Her terror-struck sometime scholar, to take
   Me sailing: Launched on the wide Beaufort River
    We tacked, I took the tiller till my mistake
Upset the sparkling scene, and we capsized.

I was baptized! But scrambled on the hull
  Not, as she'd hoped, Sea-Isle amphibian—
    Wet but what otherwise I'd always been:
   Too brazenly artistic for a man,
    Too clever for own good, bafflingly keen
On all that nonsense of the beautiful.

I longed to please, to make Lowcountry Lad,
  Highest scout-badge in our united eyes.
    Our notions differed, but our goal was one,
   Thought I: to bring me home. What a surprise
    When my scheme to attend, as she had done,
"Chas'un Cawlidge" she vetoed, who had said

All my days it was a finishing school
  For parish Geechees—half those registered
    Came from our isles; but that was changing now,

I must aim Ivy. Her ever-final word
   Propelled me to Harvard, began our slow
Tie-severing, relaxing of hawk-eyed rule.

Each time I'd home to Beaufort we'd become
   More nearly strangers. Pitiful and strange,
     That having toiled so long to simplify,
   Snip Rococo curlicues, rearrange
     Me as a sailing sipper, 'twas she, not I,
Who simplified, slipping by slow turns dumb,

That fine-honed tongue left with no wit to spare.
   Senility snatched memory in both kinds,
     Then all at once what relics mind had kept;
   Exiled in her flesh, beholden to hands
     No blood of hers—mercy she mostly slept,
Knowing nothing of who she was, or where.

If last Regatta Day in her right mind
   She'd measured me on the Sea Island Yacht
     Verandah at Rockville, where she once danced
   (Courted, may be), I trust my aunt would not
     Have nursed disappointment—me easy-stanced,
Wholly content mixing with kin and kind

(The same there), my thirst this down-home day slaked
   With beer, not beauty, not a breath of Yeats
     On my lips as I watched cousins' children sail,
   No airs, ambitions, self- and soul- debates,
     Wrapped like a vine about the rough-planed rail—
At what became of the dream-crossed boy she baked.

* The designation "Geechee" is often misunderstood to refer exclusively to Gullah speakers of African descent. It also comprehends the white descendants of Sea Island planters who can understand and often speak the language of their former servants.
** The vicinity of Spring Street, in Elliottborough on the west side of Charleston's upper peninsula, has for at least 160 years been notable as the abode of the mixed-race unofficial families of patrician white Charlestonians.

THE CLOSET SHEEP

Thinking of Cousin Blank the other Crow,
I hissed to my tumbler, "It must be so!"
No Archimedes moment, yet a beam
Through our vast cousinry's murky-bath stream:
Truth there all this time, right before mine eyes,
Classic case of overachieved disguise—
I'd vaguely wondered why he never tired
Trumpeting zest for pussy, always squired
To parties town and country the same blonde
Who on inspection wasn't, nor seemed fond
Of her dashing escort. It struck me too
His involvement with mash and barbecue
Was more *engagé*; an ageing playboy
Who pointedly read it, left airbrushed joy
Flopping about his period garçonnière.
Silly moi! Obvious now the signs were there—
Were *road*-signs, honey! Even the strained curl
Of disdain branding some wispy a "girl":
Backass psychoalgebra, plain as day,
As all such signs and portents make their way
To left of the equals, suddenly mass
Like summer coeds on Marion Square grass
Where I would join him for a lunchtime 'wich,
Listen an extra sub's worth to the itch
And tickle of expatiating lust
Scoring the nubile prospects (yes, it *must*,
But at the times—is my gaydar so lame?),
A hyper commentator on a game
Sans rules or goals.—"That one's undone her top!
That hot-sauce brunette! Those legs just won't stop!
Aargh, Cuz, catch those nuclear-warhead tits!
Bet that one swallows ... Cor, she's doing splits!"
(It did sometimes occur this talent-scout
Refereeing beaver had called time out

To join me scrubbing adjacent washboards
Of Frisbee-lobbing frat-hunks.) Life affords
So little time for being what we are,
And he nails thirty years to the wrong star—
What a waste of a queen! What was so wrong
With what he is and has been all along?
It's not as though aught of the cousinry
Would give a roach-ass—and he used to be,
Before he cased himself in that fat-suit...
And he might have...Hush, child, the issue's moot.
He graced the wrong feast, he tilled barren ground:
What profit now regret he might have found
A menu more toothsome than bottle-babe
Or mustard-based? Where was his astrolabe?

COUSIN ARCHIBALD AT SOUTH BEACH

> Then I saw the fairies dancing
> With moonlight softly glancing
> On the starry steps entrancing.
>
> —Archibald Rutledge, "The Fairies' Dance"

He'd always fancied fairies, longed to join
Their starry dance. Some sicko Carabosse
Cashed his wish, plucked him from the portico
At Hampton, where, unnoticed since his last *
Contra-dance with the Reaper some years past
Nightly he'd gargled sonnets. "Time to go."
Of guide and such strange urgency at loss
He went, assuming the command divine.

He strode into the throbbing strobe-lit scene
Expecting minuet and gossamer;
Found glistening go-go's, acres of flesh
Tanned deep as his favourite riding-crop,
Men doing things no gentleman would stoop
To whisper. What had become of his wish?
Must be sore eyes, shadows of what they were,
Sunken to sockets, hawk-prow proud between.

Surely he'd misconstrued what he'd just seen?
Invented, say—imagination's cables
Had snapped at last, spewing rank demons forth
To skim corruption from this filthy age.
Nothing so vile had sullied his pure page
These eighty books, and even "at the North"
He'd met no equal; how evil disables
The faithful heart, fouls all we reckoned clean!

Like Grandam Jane, his cousin, in her white
Gloves and pearls, perfectly understated,
Observing all the hallowed niceties—
Imperial carriage, classic grey day dress,
Of purer eyes than behold wickedness—
Stepping around Grandsire's adulteries
Down her garden path at whose end waited
A peony pleading to be staked right.

Salvific gift and crippling curse in one,
Spectacles programmed to filter out all
Untowards in that pagan temple's absurd
Gyrations, grating sound and angry light,
Body-worshippers' putrid party-night:
Our cousin moved untouched, delighted heard
The serene sweetness of the veery's call
As he walked out to a South Santee dawn.

* On the South Santee River in the parish of St. James, Santee, Hampton
Plantation was the ancestral home of Archibald Rutledge (1883–1973), who
inherited and restored the great house (ca. 1730), and wrote about it in many of
his books. The portico was added in time for President Washington's 1791 visit.

A COLOUR SCHEME

Mrs. Hugh Swinton (née Judith Simons of Middleburg; 1712–1781)
reflects during the dedication service for the new Chapel of Ease at Pompion Hill, Parish of St.
Thomas and St. Denis, in the Province of South Carolina, August 1765.

Let him drone on, I am already damned
And will take up my hell like needlework
When I sink to my pit...here, I suppose,
With Mother and Papa, not having forged
In fifty years ties stronger than those first.
I shall glide up the rivers one last time,
Oblivious to the sunset's sorcery,
Whose eyes once darted like a wren's, Hugh said,
When he still said things I'd choose to remember.
So stark the colours, this scorched pitch of season,
The mass of greens worn to moth-mumbled baize,
Houses ablaze, sizzling in sun-struck white,
Wide water's azure deepening the dome's.
Here we assemble to consecrate change,
Far as lacking bishop we may, a lack
Never felt ere, nor craved such elegance.
Another language spelt another world
When I was a child, now grown utter stranger
As Papa would have been on coming here. *
Twice losing worlds, each clean start building better.
What would he say to this? He might yet live,
Gone ninety, drooling, marble-eyed, hound-panting.
Praise God he's not who ploughed up change enough.
Now nothing French is left besides our names!
How British this grand room we dedicate,
Palladian window, pulpit palace-worthy,
Inlaid and carved as though it held the scrolls,
Not merely Mr. Garden sawing on.
Small wonder my eyes scurry to bound free
Through that new window, many-paned, high-arched,
Sash raised, so no mullions to punctuate
Yon shining stream that is alone the same,

Will be when I come cold to my last bed,
As Papa found it when all this rich parish
Was wilderness—nor hut nor fence nor field—
Reminding him, he said—I was so small,
Perhaps Peter told it me later on,
Helping me know the father I scarce had—
Of the estuary near our home in France
He fled, not quite thirteen, in deepest night,
Made outlaw, common thief in his own land—
And thirty years' industry furnished full store
For us all, the eight who would live to wed;
We would want for naught in a worldly way...
But had he lived ten years to see me wed
What could he have done to dower my heart
That marriage scarce touched—false note! More than
   touched,
Deadened like a sting. I should have remained
Spinster, grey part I've shadowed decades now,
Both children married, seldom seen, not close,
Who swallowed my bitterness with strained milk...
Now I'm relict, easier to play dried miss—
God's bounty seemed the news that he was dead **
In fact and law, as to my baffled heart
From that first winter, when he made me know
His love-gaze had been for acres to come,
And leverage. I held firm through the worst,
And siblings, bless them, sitting satisfied
Like a limb of perfectly polished crows
With this glazed, plastered, painted, carpentered
Temple lofted to their aspirations,
Loyally taking my part, ever kind
Through all the scandal and Hugh's craziness,
Though I was much to blame, daring to seize
One summer week what marriage had not brought. ***
I must feign joy at phoenix Pompion Hill,
But miss the old plain timber-framed white box,
That unadorned lost world—ah, *terre lointaine*,
The old tongue bells it true...Papa's burial,

An August noon like this, a-simmer with heat,
Cicadas chorusing in angry waves.
And now this handsome ark of Flemish bond,
With high cool cove, and a scheme for the shutters,
Beige inset with slate-grey: White would not do, ****
Plain things of my upbringing no more suit.
Next Benjamin will raise a nabob's villa,
Like Mr. Pinckney's mansion on the Bay,
Take down the simple farmhouse good enough
For my birth, as for his. He's grown so fat, *****
We all grow Roman, our tastes imperial...
How? Yes, Jamie dear, you shall have aunt's hand,
We'll stroll the wood-path home—(lopsided pair!)—
The route we used to take—turn not that stone.
What a fine dinner we shall spread this day!
The sermon nears devoutly-wished "Amen."
Patience, child, all troubles wear white in time,
Soon we shall savour sweet air and green shade.

* Benjamin Simons I (1672–1717), born on the Ile de Ré, was orphaned and swept to London in the confusion following the Revocation of the Edict of Nantes. There he was discovered by chance by a Du Pré family, relations of his mother, and brought by them to Carolina, where he married Mary Esther Du Pré in 1692 and prospered mightily.
** Long estranged from his difficult wife, Dr. Hugh Swinton (born in Edinburgh in 1705) died destitute in New York on 26 December 1759.
*** While her husband was in Charles Town on business, she succumbed to the attractions of his brother-in-law's younger brother John Stewart. Informed of the affair by his precocious daughter, Dr. Swinton attacked his cuckolder and sliced off an ear. This was the only Early Georgian sex scandal to achieve the pages of the *South-Carolina Gazette*.
**** The exterior trim of Pompion Hill Chapel had been painted uniform white for as long as anyone could remember, but during restoration begun in 2005 paint analysis revealed that some of the shutters were original, and that the 1764 colour scheme was as described. It was replicated when the exterior woodwork was repainted in 2006.
***** The plain cypress house at Middleburg Plantation, adjoining Pompion Hill on the Eastern Branch of the Cooper River, was finished by Benjamin Simons I in time for his fifth child to be born there in the spring of 1699. His daughter Judith's fears for its future were unfounded. The house was extended two bays to the east about 1800, but otherwise is almost exactly as she knew it, the oldest surviving wooden structure south of Virginia, still home to descendants of its Huguenot builder.

III. States of Mind

Life and the memory of it so compressed
they've turned into each other. Which is which?

—Elizabeth Bishop, "Poem"

VITA BREVIS

A spaghetti junction of roads not taken—
C'est moi in a not-shell! Not to blaspheme,
But it is as though Yeats' silence were broken
Only in his fifties—no pearl-pale dame,
Nor windswept reeds, nor wanderings of Oisin,
No pitched hair-tent dimming the universe...
If thirty years' struggle had never been?
Without precocious attempts to rehearse,
Limber theme and technique, could he have soared
Free of the maze love mired him in when young?
Or consider the dumb man Our Lord cured:
How often his miracle-loosened tongue
Must have pined for all the occasions when speech
Was called for and came not—facility,
Baffled, posthumous, contorting to reach
Years long inurned in silence. So with me,
Since sans preamble, not a year ago
Dumb tongue snapped shackles, Dame Kind summoned
    voice:
Grateful the tardy seed begins to grow,
Yet how resist, as I rhyme and rejoice,
Ruing that early mode of ardent dreams,
The shafts unraised to misremembered names,
Harvard songs that daringly spliced extremes,
Love lyrics posted from within the flames.

On Hearing the Latest Terrorist Threat
of Annihilation

A Babel of avian assertion
  Greets salmon sun rising like a Monet
Impression; a late October morn begun
  In mist will fair to Canaletto day.

Knowing their mist-choked boughs will soon swim clear
  Piazza-perched I scan the cloud-capped trees
And murmur thanks for peace prevailing here,
  Frail clutch of quotidian certainties

In a world whose temples and towers are now
  Hostage to whims of fanatical hate.
Fish-tail palm adds a frond, grapefruit globes glow
  Placid on my Horatian estate.

LYING IN STATE

As here I lie
In this state-chamber, dying by degrees,
Hours and long hours in the dead night, I ask
"Do I live? Am I dead?" Peace, peace seems all.
—Browning, "The Bishop Orders His Tomb"

In a rice-bed the size of a pumpkin-patch
For all whose frolicking I might have been
A courtesan unused to getting hits,
Cinderella the shoe no longer fits,
A fairy-tale retiree, deposed queen
Usurper's spies have sod-all cause to watch.

Perma-twilight of drawn double-lined drapes
With vampire fail-safe of shutters nailed fast
Filters the harsh indignities of day—
Blanche, Alex, any Lady of the Lay
Would have felt at home as, swelling the cast
Of Gothic has-beens plotting their escapes

Or Oscar comebacks, for most part have I
In this latest of the strange interludes
And long embarrassing pauses that chequer
My stellar eclipse. Each morning I stir
A touch less foreign to the attitudes
Pertaining to four-poster dignity

If not the theatrics of Lord Marchmain *
Subsiding in the Chinese Drawing-Room—
Yet from my plateau also may be seen
Some lesser-specimen *objets de Chine*,
A porcelain pillow and (dust their only bloom)
Bulbless bulb-pots. The close of Milord's reign

Curtained a way of life, indeed an age.
This house's fall, abundantly foretold
In fissures numberless, may be put off
When rich trash bags it trophy: soon enough
I shall resume my flight from winter's cold.
While it lasted, this was a fitting stage

For mine, topmost twig of a patrician tree
Once accustomed to state—and not this damp
Draught-ridden parody. Fat centuries
We pleased ourselves, and now, hushed witnesses,
All power and glory flown, we can but camp
In the leavings of our ascendancy.

* The protracted deathbed of the penultimate Marquis of Marchmain occupies most
of chapter five of Book II of Evelyn Waugh's *Brideshead Revisited*. It begins:

> "Plender, get a bed made up for me downstairs."
> "Very good, my lord. Which room shall we put it in?"
> Lord Marchmain thought for a moment. "The Chinese
> drawing-room; and, Wilcox, the 'Queen's bed.'"
> "The Chinese drawing-room, my lord, the 'Queen's bed'?"
> "Yes, yes. I may be spending some time there in the next few
> weeks."
> The Chinese drawing-room was one I had never seen used;
> in fact one could not normally go further into it than a small
> roped area round the door, where sight-seers were corralled
> on the days the house was open to the public; it was a splendid,
> uninhabitable museum of Chippendale carvings and porcelain
> and lacquer and painted hangings; the "Queen's bed," too, was
> an exhibition piece, a vast velvet tent like the Baldachino at St.
> Peter's. Had Lord Marchmain planned this lying-in-state for
> himself, I wondered, before he left the sunshine of Italy?

GREAT POSSESSIONS

> But when the young man heard that saying, he went
> away sorrowful: for he had great possessions.
>
> —Matthew 19:22

> Look, if a beggar, in fixed middle-life,
> Should find a treasure,—can he use the same
> With straitened habits and with tastes starved small,
> And take at once to his impoverished brain
> The sudden element that changes things,
> That sets the undreamed-of rapture at his hand
> And puts the cheap old joy in the scorned dust?
>
> —Browning, "Karshish"

I had them too, and they
Impeded, then imprisoned me.
Years waned before I woke to see
That I was thrall to my heaped treasure,
Innocent-seeming pleasure
In rare works of art had taken away
More joy than beauty gave—
Watchful, wakeful, anxious eye trained
On each upstart tropical wave,
Reduced to vapours every time it rained.

No less do they possess
Me now diaspora's divide
Has parceled former joy and pride
Among cousinly premises,
Store-houses, garages,
Attics, and my citadel in distress,
The once-grand drawing-room
In which for this strange interlude
I perch, take stock, and parry doom,
Straining to glimpse some hint of latitude.

The porcelains delight
No connoisseur, no more displayed;
Not a sliver of light has rayed
On the marvelous cobalt glaze
    Of the double-gourd vase
Since four months gone I tucked it out of sight,
      Bubble-swathed, in a shed.
No loving hand has lemon-oiled
My prize Stonington drop-leaf, fed
The patina for whose good health I toiled.

    The books! The other day
Rummaging through pile on pile
No use to a soul all this while
I found a mouse had made a feast
    Of my rarest Yeats first.
Though damage was done, and vain my dismay,
    I cradled what was left,
Wondering what pest had gnawed apart
Which other gem, feeling bereft
And helpless, stricken to my shaken heart.

    The pictures most of all!
A remnant beaming pleasure still,
Guests on the walls of Cousin Will,
Who cherishes much as I did;
    But half of his are hid
For lack of space against a closet wall.
    The silver, black as death,
Relique of social poetry,
Slumbers abased eclipse beneath
Another cousin's matrimonial *lit.*

Yes, the daubs wound me most,
For they were my chief glory once,
Albeit the uncontrolled expense
That undermined my house of cards—
The aesthete disregards,
When beauty swells the heart, constraints of cost.
Now stacked five deep, they peer
Accusingly, and seem to hiss,
"What sorry pass has brought us here?
Have we offended? Do we merit this?"

My supreme possession
Shroud-muffled apes a parlour-chair
In the *lointaine* of yesteryear
When state-rooms were sheet-jacketed
And all white locals fled
City heat for island estivation.
I fail of nerve to face
Guardi's great scene queer quirk made mine:
Why draw him down to my disgrace,
For all his exaltation of decline?

Sublime capriccio,
His soaring-arched, light-suffused court
Once faced a fitting counterpart,
A luminous Sam Bough sunset
That each clear evening met
Its image in the drawing-room window
Fronting the very spot,
A Fife harbour, the wide prospect
That sold the house I left to rot
For *vita nuova* fecklessly wrecked.

Bough glows reproachfully
Like the coal-fire ages unlit
In the grate 'gainst which I propped it.
Consign the stashed loot to the flames?
My better angel shames
Mere thought of such a scorched-earth remedy
For Gordian impasse.
Ironist above his station,
Sam reflects in protective glass
Present poverty and vacillation.

A shell-shocked refugee
From an abortive life, I long
To redress some of what went wrong—
Or is it base impulse to slope
Off that kindles new hope
In plans to retrace travels that took me
To heights untasted since?
They forestall all such schemes, dead weight
However fair. Put off pretence,
Admit the heart can change, the hour is late,

The option may not last.
Treasures tie up the capital
That freed might make dreams possible,
Purchase freedom to cultivate
Talents that blossomed late
And quaff from wells but tasted in the past:
Mysterious Torcello,
Douce Devon, Sligo, bleak Caithness,
Whose unseen Boreal afterglow
Smoothes promise over present-tense distress.

Divest before you hate,
Sell the objects to which you gave
Lavish love to others who crave
As once you did, who will delight
In your wake. It is right
So to do, maybe it is not too late
To venture untried ways,
After a lifetime of false starts
Consecrate my remaining days
To living, that most demanding of arts.

A NEST

From the life of an ultramontane saint—
The limb a beast gnawed years ago sewn back:
Miraculously whole, I pad barefoot,
Tickled by hardwood's flowing grain, still not
Believing this seismic outbreak of luck,
This rich rejoinder to prolonged complaint.

All those months on the run, footsore exile
Trailing his pilgrim-pack from one brief haven
To next, tasting no continuing city,
Ever more down at heart, cursing Fate's shabby
Scything of the good things fat years had given...
As I turn tasks unattempted this long while.

Hanging clothes in a closet, stacking washed T's
In a real chest of drawers, giving a friend
The address I have again, at least *pro tem*—
All so wondrous strange!—as not at the time
I feel how weary I was, what a wound
Gapes from the bruit of sharp exigencies.

My partisans, new haven's host among,
Voice hopes this pocket of security
Prove fertile ground for art—and I assure
Them there is nothing I now desire more
Than to squeeze the rind of my time bone-dry,
Crafting songs wastrel midlife left unsung.

This table set in a south-facing bay
Commands a small walled garden's green swirl
Through which pours light so heavenly pure it seems
Never to have beheld the want that numbs,
Care that coils will, will centre this new world,
Help me to harvest words with which to pay

For price-pearl fortune of one more fresh start,
A chance to order my house, perchance to seize
Some of that light to mitigate the gall
Of frequent flight, and steady hand to fill
A few more moulds, cast in iambic bronze
Sorrows untold that flood my failing heart.

A HANGING JURY

For Will

In course of half an hour, and less than three
    Fat fingers of best batch, deft hand remakes
Room and outlook of one sapped refugee.
    A dozen nails and hooks are all it takes:
Wiped months of eclipse propped insultingly
    Next skirting-boards, arraigned like found-out fakes—
Proud pictures beam majestic soon as hung.
What a feast of old friends eyes dance among!

A blur of snap decisions! Which way go
    This not quite pair? Say wall beside the door?
Chapman's *Whitby* on top, yes, and *Godstow*,
    Anon, beneath. Lest tint-blanching sun pore
Over paper, I must calculate. No—
    Harm's slant, dawn-shaft. Let's try an oil with more…
Above that chair? Robust enough, yes: there,
Territory awarded the Lorimer.

Of sunset, oddly. Yet not, now I think,
    Sitting to ponder your juxtapositions,
You having run out of nails, downed one drink
    And gone, promising to make good omissions
Another night. How well those pendants link
    To anchor the grandest of my Venetians,
The giraffe-arched Guardi *capriccio*,
Finest in private hands for aught I know,

Whose sacrifice would set me up for life—
    Or residue. Towards fateful auction-block
Temptation creeps: one gavel-tap to knife
    All ganged financial furies and unlock
Sunset feathered as those salmon-piped Fife
    Clouds Lorimer floats! Now I can take stock
Once more of treasures the option revives:
Guardi would see me through a brace of lives!

I envision the bare-walled space that waits
    At land's end in my cherished Southernmost,
Where pretty ones will emerge from their crates,
    I from worst nightmare of loved city lost,
Consumed by greed. If no grace compensates
    So foul a theft, I may, long tempest-tossed,
Achieve a haven where I can recruit
And coax a little end-of-season fruit.

Behind my field-desk, you anticipate
    That final shuffling of worldlies before
Eyes' friends fade to inventoried estate:
    Below, the Verner I've come to love more
Since I dwelt in etched subject, and wall-mate,
    Where with dancer's upsurge thrust nobly soar
Cyclopean limbs of a Walter Locke
Longleaf Titan of uncompromised stock,

Such as one singles in the endless waves
    Of pine and sky below St. Augustine—
The halfway stretch between this nest of knaves,
    Change-cozened Charleston, and the *laissez* scene
Every fibre of untuned being craves:
    You poise an emblematic go-between
To goad resolve, and when launched scheme lands right,
Trump pine with Townsend Morgan's *Key West Bight*,

Unglazed, chest-tombed, useless as these have lain
    Till sharp eye and skilled hand joined to redeem
Months' numb-heart camping-out. While daubs remain
    I'll hail you, cos, for making halfway seem
Almost a home—soon, pray, to sail again
    En route to that blank room of fervent dream,
Where I shall seek your aid, and one less nail,
To embellish the curtain-chapter of my tale.

MUTUAL ADVANTAGE

As I straighten a skyscraper book-stack
Out you dart on a ledge of Huguenot
Transactions to ray me with somnolent
Indignation—what quake of fell intent
Disturbed the nest you had disposed just so?
What tenant wouldn't be taken aback?

'Twas not premeditate malignity,
But ignorance I sheltered such a guest.
Gold when you freeze in martyred rectitude,
Slowly you green as I berate my rude
Intrusion on your space, culpas oil-pressed
In coaxing tones I trust fall soothingly.

You're welcome to my cot, and to accept
Assurances I shall not touch said pile
All winter, all yours by this quitclaim deed:
Startled in turn, I find you meet a need
Dimly asserting itself this long while,
A chafing lacuna to which I kept

Returning without tugging into focus
Till now: companionship, estate for which,
Youth's repertoire and expectations shrunk,
Naught in romantic love left to debunk,
Sensible older folks, right side of rich,
Settle, emotional Gulf Coast—all hocus

Of passion spent, or that fund never tapped.
This, friend, is, as they bark, win-win: *You* need
My central heat, I should embrace the chance,
When crossed in mortaring phrasework, to glance
Up instinctive appeal you haste to heed—
Your sage eye opens above the grin wrapped

Inscrutable about that sculpted prow,
Welcome confirmation some life persists
Outwith the mind, even for me. Compose
Your Hancock-flourish tail, back off now, close
Bold eye, slink back to sleep. Byzantine twists,
Fortuna! Our disparities somehow

Transcend grotesque: My hunger mirrors yours,
A little warmth. We'll get on famously,
Each with his claim to make, his gift to bring,
And dreaming of its coming inch towards spring,
When from cold's coils we shall once more be free,
Or easier in the illusion out of doors.

AN IRRESOLUTE THRUSH

Ranked septs of your clan proclaim
   By choral cry, scything wing,
And mating dance cycle come
   Through damps to threshold of spring.

You perch aloof from glad din,
   Impassive on peeling paling,
Oblivious of swelling sun
   Enraptured neighbours are hailing.

You risk no response at all.
   I take your demeanour's hint,
Recoiling as from the gall
   Of a personal affront.

Mute thrush, you emblematize
   My decades of glacial waste,
When trick was to temporize,
   And folly discounted cost:

With riches to plumb and give,
   All-cautious of stepping wrong,
Afraid to leap into love,
   Fearful to stretch into song.

THE FIRST ANNIVERSARY

(29 April 2005)

For months aware I'd wish to keep this day
    But knowing not with what solemnities,
I lolled a leisured progress that made way
    To the "Parrot" to toast in barside ease
Annus Mirabilis, perhaps essay
    Charting the changes wrought by this new lease,
Sudden re-emergence alive and strong
Of a decades-despaired-of gift for song.

Venue entirely apt, as soon occurred,
    For the miracle happened in a bar,
A lingered-over lunchtime lager stirred
    The buried talent to spectacular
Afterlife, as word by rapid-fire word
    A verse sprang forth, then in what seemed bizarre
Coincidence, or sheer resumer's luck,
That very night a second lyric struck.

The next few weeks confirmed belated bloom
    No cruel tease, but prologue to much fruit—
At last my caverned Alph had burst his tomb
    To sparkle in kind sun and prosecute
Vengeance on silence and heart-stifling gloom,
    Refreshing spirit to remotest root,
Delighting parched encouragers with more
And yet more songs to plateau at fourscore.

Work of a score compacted in one year!
    Not quenched but fueled by another glass,
Amazement blazed and settled to sincere
    Awed gratitude ripeness should come to pass
So long past expectation, reappear
    Beaconing me out of mezzanine morass
To sunny uplands of satisfied toil,
Anointing my hand with metrical oil.

Later that day a hazy 'prentice queen
	Over a tincture happened to let fall
Some bird thought extinct, that no one had seen
	For aeons, was back. He couldn't recall
The name, but thought the last sighting had been—
	In the Forties...? "Forty-four?" "Know-it-all,
How'd you—?" As I cried out with tearful thrill,
"Then it was—it *is*—the Ivory-Bill!"

Irrevocably consigned to past tense,
	Blot on our stewardship greed-guilt rubbed raw,
Getting on with existence in immense
	Viridian chasms of Arkansas!
Smile messenger assumes due recompense
	Greets glimpsed correlative—my voice's thaw
Was even so a death-warrant reversed,
Sweet water welling to enfeebled thirst.

May I fence well the woods in which my gift
	Flourished unnoticed like that great-winged bird
While I passed a Romantic's span adrift
	In self-pity; by this miracle spurred,
Muse-blessed in latter reaches likewise lift
	Suffused with joy a song so long unheard,
His two-note call enlarged to leitmotif—
The triumph of faith over unbelief.

Grant, Muse, my song, having like his a home
	And present tense, may live to celebrate
Other returns of the day one thought dumb
	Burst into music! Life once desiccate
Rounds as trickle of lyrics is become
	Frothing spate; my harvest begun so late,
So many unsown seasons to requite,
May I scythe cheerfully far into the night.

ST. BLANCHE

Stanley: Delicate piece she is.
Stella: She is. She was.

—*A Streetcar Named Desire,* Scene 8

As your cell-mate sister in the past tense
  I love you, darling, more than ever now,
Having adored Dame Blanche the aeons since
  First teen fling, little imagining how
I should one day become your breath-smudged glass—
Not in lubricity! I never was

Drawn to, or dab at, that, rather the sense
  Of having outlived one's world, for I feel
By cosmic fluke, or joke at vast expense,
  I am cast torchère of a beau ideal
No other denizen can understand.
My home, like yours, lies in a vanished land.

And you were pure, your whoredom decked with lies
  Cried beauty was what really drove your heart;
Truest when not, your foolishness was wise,
  If Elysian conceit fenced you apart.
You bathed and tried to prettify your hell—
Tawdry the effect, but the impulse was well.

At length you sharpened steel to pierce *their* lies;
  Your truth their "one unforgivable thing,"
You had to be consigned. No local tries
  That caper yet with me, but ere jaws spring
I aim like you, if sans bouclé, to say
"I'm only passing through," and swish away

To the town your creator, high and antic,
   The winter you prepared to go onstage
Found and loved first taste, your kind of romantic,
   And there this numbing otherness assuage:
Where no one's bothered what or who you do,
Any old wreck can weep and pray to you.

Making Pimento Cheese While
the Quarter Drowns

Struck by trapped wretches clinging for their lives
As waters swirl and smack and lick the eaves,
I inventory my crisis resorts—
Rather the plural that ceaselessly laves
This submersible life. My spar of sorts

No anchored gable but feather of Crow,
Yet beyond the whole plucked bird, what will do,
Who tugs from the brink, speeds consolation,
When dark waters congregate to swallow
Me and mine, what can I steady mind on?

The friend, first off, whose feathers outsheen Crow's,
Sure of aim, majestic-winged: Blessèd Muse!
To have clambered out of crater or eye
With sleek-leaved dittie-sprig—would that not rouse
Trampled spirit to utter joyful cry?

But wordsmith Alp-leaps are matched smile for smile
By kitchen-stints concocting treat or meal
(If no more certain than song of a taker),
Grating pungent cheddar in wide-lipped bowl,
Reducing diced pepper in wine vinegar,

Blending old familiar tunes—bliss amid
Slings and arrows that season my scotched hide.
Cocktail nibbles when I've no notion where
My pillow-stone will next take up abode?
Finger-food is tastier fare than despair.

A certain romance invests the *ad hoc*.
If cooking be largely a matter of luck,
Fortune favours respecters of details.
I grant my faithful Muse the better cook;
Her specials never spoil when power fails.

"We Have a Gospel to Proclaim"

Indeed we have, and hymns to help us tote
Unwieldy joy. That one I've often sung;
Its tune circles my head, threatening to land
In my throat as I writhe to understand
What I witnessed just now. Somnolent young
Refusing God's gift tined a leaden note

To skew the calm of bland September morn!
Like angels guarding gates of Paradise
Thwart each entrance the Gideons offered
Lizard-green Testaments, "the engraftèd word,
That is able to save souls"—quel surprise,
Reactions ranged from indifference to scorn.

Not one changed hands. Wishing their witness well,
I pray vinyl-cased seed may chance to fall
On some good ground, but that route cannot go,
Haunting campus and corners—goodness no,
I could no more pummel pulpit or bawl
"Je-sus!" from a box than turn infidel.

Mixtures of method, medium, motive
Marble proclamation like other arts;
Mine is all but soundless—not scratch of pen
But hand brushing downpage as words fall in,
Faint echo of the Word's power to touch hearts,
To shake and shape hearkeners where they live.

May I sing Gospel even when I sound
To preach the low text of self-absorption:
I watch my pocket-world not in belief
It matters greatly, nor to pump relief
To my vexed heart, nor tout what I have done,
But to commend the comfort I have found

Striving to walk in faith in a faithless age
Whose embarrassed young hands brusquely decline
Abundant life. And if I seldom speak
Plainly of faith it is not far to seek—
Keeping faith with gifts motivates each line,
The lamp of scripture backlights every page.

They work their work, I mine. Unto all lands *
We are bid bear good news till all have heard.
Clarity of purpose and well-wrought speech
Grant, Lord, that through this vessel life may reach
At least one soul that would not take the Word
Direct from these brothers' well-meaning hands.

* The allusion is to Tennyson's "Ulysses," lines 33–43, when the speaker
acknowledges that his son Telemachus is utterly unlike him but admirable in his way.
The verse paragraph concludes:

> Most blameless is he, centred in the sphere
> Of common duties, decent not to fail
> In offices of tenderness, and pay
> Meet adoration to my household gods,
> When I am gone. He works his work, I mine.

TIME-OUT AT APPOMATTOX

When schism loomed, feeling like Crazy Jane
    Dishing her bishop Swiftian Like-it-was,
I told our chief the resemblance was plain
    To moss-mustached old colonel of Lost Cause
Waked *circa* Nineteeen-Three to gird again,
    Convinced the bitter end was but a pause,
Exhorting long-dead recruits to the van:
"To Cemetery Ridge! I have a plan!"

So where were you when Pike brandished crozier, *
    Donned mitre calling God Himself old hat,
At best a clapped-out metaphor, rosier
    Bliss-dawn of sex and drug Jehosaphat
Rendering resurrection daily dozier—
    On to the Prayer Book! You slept through all *that*
To swagger Monday-morning fiddleback **
Forty years after you balked at attack?

The barn-door dust, belatedly you rouse
    To cry anathema Gene's turncoat dick ***
Pokes no mirror of your missionary spouse!
    Screw reconciliation, Father, pick
Propitious quarrel, rending hallowed house
    To advance your chances of a bishopric:
Give me the Egyptian hippo-deity
Ere your homophobic hypocrisy.

* James Pike (1913–1969), fifth bishop of Northern California, 1958–1966; in the 1960s the Episcopal Church repeatedly declined to prosecute him for heresy for denying such basic doctrines as the Trinity and the Virgin Birth.
** A chasuble (the garment worn over alb and stole when a priest celebrates the Eucharist) whose front is shaped like a violin.
*** The consecration of openly gay Gene Robinson as Bishop of New Hampshire destroyed the fragile detente between factions within the Episcopal Church.

AUTUMN IN EVERYTHING

> And autumn grows, autumn in everything.
> —Browning, "Andrea del Sarto"

For David

Harvest-home tints in the Berwickshire dales
  Sloping to Gala suffuse morn's first note
    Observing with Brahmsian wistfulness
    Response to season-shift grows more acute
      As we ascend in years. Why should the loss
Of leaves strike so when our own sap-fount fails?

The cause, I suppose—we wax conscious of
  The major transition to which we tend;
    My season now, autumn will soon be yours.
    These latter cycles how my hand has strained
      To pick talent's first-fruits hid all these years,
Distilling art against my own remove.

Yet urgency never quite tastes the blade.
  Scotia's sharp turns of season baffle mind,
    For all I weathered nigh a hundred there.
    Here at the tropics' north edge I have found
      Evergreen continuities assure
More time than like to tick before I fade.

Grandmother Sarah blooms to mind, a smile
  Fixed on folded hands on Upcountry hill
    As she eyed the maples flanking her perch,
    Pronouncing them "red, *red!*" when magical
      Flame-tongues outflew vocabulary's reach
In one late missive to ivied exile.

Fear it was not—that was none of her line—
  But surely suspecting each time her last
    She lived out that "continual farewell"
  Of Yeats, understood unread, senses tensed *
      Each parting to fill my image with oil
Enough to keep it lit through days' decline.

Once more I stand before her flaming trees
　　As thirty years shrink to an eye-blink's pause
　　Our earthly love locked live by sacred trust;
Loving like her what I am poised to lose,
　　I garner frost-menaced harvest to last
Long winters after our snuffed images.

* "Before us lies eternity; our souls/Are love, and a continual farewell." "Ephemera,"
ll. 23–24; *Crossways* (1889).

Bodily Decrepitude

Is wisdom, improbably asserts Yeats *
  Who for a Viagra-vial would have flogged
Nobel, and did for ur-. We sever mates— **
  For this survivor what has sagged has sagged,

Desire's discounted, I've no wish to swagger
  A sempiternal stud, merely to keep
The lamp lit in my mind as flesh-walls stagger
  And I shuffle singing towards long sleep.

If but one of my knees is "medieval," ***
  The Quasimodo lurch proceeding thence,
As painful to walk as to watch, has proved withal
  (As we say) "a learning experience"—

Chiefly from the gawks and grossed-out averts
  Of a college library's brutish crew
As I tilt to my feet—it almost hurts
  More to endure revulsion than pursue

Resurrection from computer console,
  Or list like sinking tanker to sought text:
Locomotion becomes heroic goal,
  Not whether but what will fall apart next

My constant study as unwatched I see
  The same flat refusal to locate themselves
In time that once gilded my panoply
  Of arrogance. Who among these young craves

Truth more than pleasure? Why should wisdom be
  Seconded to serve flesh instead of soul,
Mere aching lack, shamed incapacity
  To blaze as at prime a prodigal fool?

* "Bodily decrepitude is wisdom: young / We loved each other and were ignorant."—Yeats, "After Long Silence."
** He spent part of his Nobel Prize award on monkey-gland injections, which were reputed to restore virility. Apparently the results were disappointing.
*** "I sink on medieval knees."—Yeats, "The Municipal Gallery Revisited."

THE LUMBERJACK IN US ALL

"His galluses were down, and his
belly bulged like a sow's..."
—Charles F. Price

For Phillip Powell

Something to be said for, if not seen in,
  Letting it all flop, jellyroll at last,
Unchained belly swelling like prize pumpkin,
  Shameless surrender stapled to the mast,

Joying in low-carb tyranny's eclipse,
  Cringing no more in the shadow of salad,
Pigging on fudge brownies and sour-cream dips—
  Riddance to cuisine improving and pallid!

Burying vain essays at disinterring
  Shape of sixteen, beautiful without toil;
How liberating to voyage past caring,
  To have no patch of beauty left to spoil!

Dreading no more stern Doctor Cardio
  Behind the arras of each indulgence!
Sweet release of axing the whole drag show,
  Oozing unburdened towards deliquescence!

As I sketch Good Ship Mu-mu's sunset tack,
  A tennis Adonis in captain's white
Sprints past, slicing my cast potato-sack.
  Perhaps I shall jog round the Pond tonight.

A Clean Heart and a Right Honourable Spirit

For the Rt. Hon. The Earl of Gowrie

You would have no cause to remember me,
    Drop of the final wave
Of Harvard Wasps' drain-sucked ascendancy
    To whom you briefly gave
Instruction in the Lowellian twilight,
    Since which we have not met.
But years later, when you took a sharp right
    To grace the Cabinet
I sent good wishes, daring to surmise
    Dear dead Robert would be
Vastly amused, and much to my surprise
    You answered charmingly
On portcullis-paper. Second Thatcher,
    That long-occluded dawn!
From which you emerged with unshrunk stature
    Sailing serenely on
Through auction seas until I quite lost sight
    Of your strato-career,
But knew you were lapping sweetness and light.
    By chance I came to hear
You have a new heart. Steeped in the music
    Of King James and Cranmer,
I take their doses of heavenly physic
    Exhorting us to stir
Up or renew spirits, create within
    Clean hearts, but never guessed
Figurative pep-talk might issue in
    Carving of stricken breast.
No one I knew had cashed the metaphor
    On operating-table.
Surpassing strange impasse, to have at core
    No heart at all! Signs stable,

They stitch the donor muscle into place
    And it begins to pump
Your coroneted blood of chiefly race,
    Leavening the spent lump
Of your exhausted frame to live once more!
    The like I could not do;
What hunger you must have had to restore
    Lost vigour, to wince through
Agonies spelt in a "harrowing" group
    Premiered at a festival
Last June. Dominie, what will we not stoop
    To for crisp material?
Who'd have imagined you'd prove pioneer?
    Take my loyal salute—
To mill unfathomable pain and fear
    Through your lifelong pursuit
Of order, finding a vein that renews
    Your body and our genre,
Worthy work, acceptable to the Muse,
    Heroic double-entendre!
You've found confessional frontiers beyond
    Drink, madness, lust, divorce,
Furrows the fevered bard, our one shared bond,
    Tilled with exhausting force.
My lord, I wish you joy of your new heart.
    Faith in your gift unshaken,
May you find it pumps new life to your art,
    Rewarding high risk taken.

THE PULITZER CHEESE-BALL

A hit I was, but not for well-sprung rhymes,
Mobbed at the interval by partisans
Of my cheese-ball! Bright rack ringing Parnassus,
Superlatives wreathed the vanishing mound,
Soon excavated to the last mite, found
A must by massed samplers. "Hon, you surpass us
All! Best ball I done had."—My chief of fans,
Cinderella. Finger food for our times!

And what a reflection on them, not one
Word about my words, but torrents anent
Wonder de-bowled and rolled in no time flat.
My plate stared blank as virgin legal pad,
But songs, it seems, were not the best they'd had.
How might mere iambs rise to rival *that*?
Roll rhymes in chopped pecans? Spice sentiment
With garlic (minced)? Inject a little fun?

That being what they want, who crave punch-lines,
Purse at subtleties, in it for the laugh
And high-carb cracker-smothering quick fix.
Hard enough as it is to craft, what hope
Of chopping Muse to squeeze to suit their scope?
As well trade in one's art for trained-dog tricks
As tailor high music to dolts who quaff
Miller Lite, and seek only highway signs.

Toss the odd ball to open-mic circuses,
Wow groundlings at the halftime chow-down show,
But segregate blest Muse from savouries,
Reserving your treasure for the fit few
Who can catch what you endeavour to do,
Whose well-tuned ears you would not blush to please,
Who, green remnant in null wasteland, yet know
Verse-farming for the lofty calling it is.

A Porlockian Débacle*

At furthest frontier of sleep,
   A Cellini lyric's sheen:
Volcanic-plug castle-keep
   Astounding prosaic plain.

I threaded its vaulted gleams,
   Testing splayed-star ribs for stress:
Yes, this was fabric of dreams,
   Jeweled yet diaphanous,

Crisp lines graved precisely right,
   Intaglio-intertwined.
I stammered in flushed delight,
   "This dittie's light-years beyond

Any song shaped heretofore!"
   But as I sat up to seek
Pen, paper, knock at front door
   Tumbled the whole fantastic

Extravagance of vision.
   Facet-flakes pitted stunned air
As I cursed fell intrusion
   And opened on—no one there?

Not the ghost of an excuse
   For masterwork aborted!
No line escaped! Total loss!
   Centuries would not have sorted

Shards to piece one phrase to tease
   Memory and expectation
Like first golden bubble's kiss
   In just-filled flute's elation.

If sunburst as such a glass,
Howso refulgent my day
It would wear the shadow-gloss
Of Heaven-sent song sped away.

---

* When in 1816 Coleridge published, at Lord Byron's urging, his glittering fragment "Kubla Khan," he gave an account of the poem's composition at a remote farmhouse between Porlock and Linton, on the Exmoor edge of Somerset, in the summer of 1797. Having taken opium, he fell asleep and dreamt an immense poem: "On awaking he appeared to himself to have a distinct recollection of the whole, and taking his pen, ink, and paper, instantly and eagerly wrote down the lines that are here preserved. At this moment he was unfortunately called out by a person on business from Porlock, and detained by him above an hour, and on his return to his room, found, to his no small surprise and mortification, that though he still retained some vague and dim recollection of the general purport of the vision, yet, with the exception of some eight or ten scattered lines and images, all the rest had passed away like the images on the surface of a stream into which a stone has been cast, but, alas! without the after restoration of the latter!" It is doubtful whether even S.T.C. himself believed this tale, but the Person from Porlock has become the most celebrated bogeyman in English poetry.

TROUVÉE

A minuscule Brancusi!
  More eye-delighting than bronze
Or polished beech its woozy
  Tide-lines of elbowing glaze—

A Sung vase, all crazing-veins
  And caramel tongues of fire
Licking ancient water-stains;
  I flip bowed facets and stare

As into winter-night blaze,
  Seeking in mesmeric glow
The bloom heat wrought to this pass—
  But spring is so long ago,

Vain to imagine as youth!
  Praise be, as I totter hence
And shadow swallows my path,
  Red buckeye strows recompense.

A SLICE OF LIME

Though the drained glass wants attending, eye lingers
Rapt over a beached lime. So many props
Of deeply-rutted rituals remain
Unexamined—if thirst did not complain,
I might contemplate this until sun drops,
Least likely of association-stringers.

Onshore-combed treeline where viridian rind
Turns pith: Edisto of an August noon.
Then a hint of feather-border technique
On Leeds creamware, nervous strokes' hide-and-seek
Like diagrammed laughter, organic rune
Shaping a text no scholarship might find.

When I twirl the glass in south-window light
Sun sprinkles through darkling rind's myriad pits
Discs of dazzle, miniatures of sunstruck
Magnolia-leaf reflections' sparklings stuck
In sermon-drone sidebar—palpable hits,
Shaming the Padre's homiletic blight.

Perched arkwise atop a mound of fused cubes,
Fortuitously (if anything be)
Bent into slope of an amphitheatre.
Epidauros, Ephesus, sites that once were
On dream-list, but I no more long to see:
Greek rusted shut, sheered sea-legs down the tubes—

No more grand voyages, at most day-jaunts.
From safe-haven London of oldest friends,
I might venture to Claremont to admire
A grassy copy. This stage I aspire *
Not to marble wonders at empires' ends;
Quite lost my eye-tooth for the scale that daunts.

As time tapers, I'm more at home each day
With close-range miracles—the present slice.
Now to drown in another amber wave
Of eighty proof parched theatre that gave
A performance itself well worth the price
Of Persian fruit—a classic, as we say.

Refill accomplished, I am armed to toast
Armchair acuity partnering mind
Like parents' persistent, curious still,
Alert, observant, all the steep downhill
Delighted each diurnal arc to find
New-chalked marvel raising an elder's ghost.

On Mother's final afternoon, she sat
Bartering breath, intent on folding dusk,
Delving fresh terms to phrase fast-falling snow
Beyond words magical. May I also
Step hence rasping praise, leaving no spent husk
To mourn sense of wonder. A glass to that.

* The famous garden of Claremont in Surrey was laid out for Lord Clare, later First
Duke of Newcastle, from 1715. The unique grass amphitheatre created by Charles
Bridgeman in about 1726, later covered with trees and shrubs by "Capability" Brown
in his radical makeover for Lord Clive, has been restored by the National Trust,
who purchased the neglected property in 1975 and have achieved an astonishing
resurrection of what was once one of the most celebrated gardens in Europe. An
article by Tim Richardson on the ongoing restoration, "The Kit-Cat at Claremont,"
appeared in *Country Life*, Vol. CXCIX, No. 46, 17 November 2005, pages 56–59;
the amphitheatre is illustrated on page 58.

IV. KEY WEST

Swiftly in the nights,
In the porches of Key West,
Behind the bougainvilleas,
After the guitar is asleep,
Lasciviously as the wind,
You come tormenting,
Insatiable.

—Wallace Stevens, "O Florida, Venereal Soil"

GONE WITH THE WIND

Once more we wait and watch and fret and wait.
As steering-currents dart and fork tonguewise
Projected-path cones' whirring blurs all eyes
Reckoning losses we might not survive
Or wish to, lives stripped bare like trees. Watch, fret,
And wait for fresh coordinates at five.

I image my southernmost city razed,
Gaffed heart's Calais, but mind declines to swatch
Blanks where my happy pencil raced to catch
Glints of pure magic mined in middle age
At long road's end. How could all that be waste,
Void as a virgin sketchpad's unturned page?

Imagination slips and fails, as friends
Assure me my loved isle would rise once more
From dreck and ashes, come what lurks in store
In cone and currents—but comforts sicken
In grim awareness my phoenix ascends
Each birth more like rotisserie chicken—

Blackened, creaking by rote. So I suppose
Reflex would stoop to pick some pieces up
And my good angel steel me not to stop
To elegize the layered slate swept clean,
But trust that when all we most cherished goes
Enough love's left to oil the sad machine.

The Wrong Sea

I.P.M. James Ingram Merrill

> Wherever that thought led,
> Turning the loose knob onto better-late-
> Than-never light, we breasted its deepening stream
> Along with others who've a date
> With sunset.
>
> —James Merrill, "Clearing the Title"

With your life and works parked in mind's foreground
  This age, strange I never noticed till now
    That you commenced wintering in Key West
The year my mad-method divining found
    Summer haven in a North Sea craw's nest.
  First charmed Lammas noons at harbour-wall's prow
I lapped your verse, whose changes rang in me
Like the improbable azure of that sea.

"The Fire Screen" and "The Summer People" spoke
  Most to me—had I seen, prophetically:
    I too would try to turn a summer place
Year round when my career went up in smoke.
    You picked a spot where summer's genial rays
  Shone always, while my grim ubiquity,
Winter, soon changed your metaphor's estate:
Screen tamed the driftwood hissing in the grate.

Chattering, I marveled how you conveyed
  Places you'd come to love, were soon to do
    In the baroque tints of your sunset phase.
You swam and rhymed beneath trade-touseled shade,
    I shivered and heaped immetrical praise
  On the stark beauty of my harbour view:
Each short bright day, chilled to my Southern core,
I loved the North Sea's icy azure more.

Cold was all I knew. If, like you, I'd found
  The Southernmost then, I'd have strobed my awe
    In bars, at parties, not just on the page;
My dumb Muse might have flowered in that ground,
    Your fulgent wake—yet cold suited my stage
  In love, the seemingly retrograde thaw
Whereby I blazed what I blush to recall,
Dispensing my musty favours to all.

I chose the wrong sea, squandering my prime
  On false gods and goals, undermining health
    In excesses by no strained stretch glamourous.
Fraction of that underutilized time
    Multiplied by hindsight ever-clamourous...
  Ah, Dives had his answer! I had wealth
Sufficient for a foothold in Key West:
Shall I Pangloss map-mangling for the best?

Both mind and body might have flourished there,
  Opened to heat like all I could not grow
    In heart or on my window-sill in Fife.
By now I should have died—so much is clear—
    But then I might have seized a larger life
  Than this guttering with starveling fruit to show
For talents lent. Patron shade, bid me come
And daub my sunset in your swansong home!

Esthétique du Mal:
Amateur Night at KWest for Men

> Fool, do not boast;
> Thou canst not touch the freedom of my mind
> With all thy charms, although this corporal rind
> Thou hast immanacled, while Heav'n sees good.
>
> —Milton, *Comus*

In a Duval dive, an apple-cheeked dancer—
All four rare gems, a first-water parure,
A reversible Irish stable-lad
Whose marketability strikes me sad
Even as whore eye applauds *con brio*:
When every inch is shared, what's left to show?

No mystery he, but my response remains
Profoundly cloaked, despite important pains
To class it admiration, not desire:
How is it poor heart so stumbles, unsure
Where eye's most certain, stammers to deny
Its own inscrutable transparency?

And when those apples have at length been plucked
By Time, not all the customers they tricked,
What will survive but honeyed memory
Of a diamond strung between gulf and sea,
Spirit capricious planets realigned
To strut a season its corporal rind?

O Jacuzzi, Thou Art Sick!

"Uncontrollably tossed on one of my surges of certitude."
—Henry James, *The Sacred Fount*

Afroth as usual with beanstalking steam
Pawing nippy night air by starts and fits,
This cauldron regilds lilies: All emerge,
Kissed by some disco-diva demiurge,
Praxitelean, leastways with lifted tits—
Flesh flawless, without seam, our fondest dream.

The jets it seems work customed wizardry
On huddled misters yearning for lost youth.
I sit next one that pares my shop-soiled flesh
Like very fruit knife, and inhale the fresh
Sensation like aroma as, forsooth,
My turnip limbs resume lost pliancy.

By the far ledge, quell polychrome nymphet,
Silken shoulders breasting the restless rack—
A hydrofoil that knows its destination.
Am I that port? Spite of sensory inflation,
I loll confounded by a gnawing lack,
The unvoiced note of one annealing jet

Silent amid the swish-swirl and limp shrieks
Of Hotlantans who know not what to do
Mouth-wise, till crisis boils, and then can funnel
Unskinned shoats—subtle charm of channel tunnel!
Ledge-dweller cometh, easing his wares through
The Georgian gaggle, knowing whom he seeks.

It grows harder to climb down to crass facts
Of sex, the more one sinks into its swim—
A failure of moral plumbing no hand
Can fix; nor can lust's fiat countermand
Revulsion at buffed hybrids of the gym;
Yesteryear's knockout no longer attracts.

Time wants to crochet images and brood!
Yet absent that stilled jet, how shall I purge
Doubts' silt? Our revels' impresario,
Where art thou, handyman? Adjust the flow,
That I may bronco-burst a sudden surge
Of certitude! Oh *la*! That *does* feel good.

AN AZURE TABULA

All island round libations of *leche*
Send heavenward through swift-mustering heat
From bustling cantinas whose shed-roof tin
Returns with interest freshly-minted sun
Streamers of laud for another rare day,
One more second chance not to cast away
So pure a gift, scatter it like the coin
Of many an elder promise-radiant dawn
That long ere nightfall swept the scrawl-fouled slate
Fizzled confused as doubt snuffed serene ray.

ANOTHER PLANET

I'd like to get away from earth awhile
And then come back to it and begin over.
May no fate willfully misunderstand me
And half grant what I wish and snatch me away
Not to return.

> —Robert Frost, "Birches"

Frost was decades from visiting Key West
When he shaped those lines, but I like to think
They lit rueful remembrance when at last
His train steamed down the Overseas, and struck
By their hint of unheeded prophecy—
For his frame hideyhole on Caroline
Is planets from any America he
Had known or rhymed before his wife's decline
And his weak lungs brought them to winter warmer.
In the early-shift Green Parrot, on high,
Unwatched, Weather Channel chamfers a corner,
Wafting an air of irreality ...
Correction sustained: lily-gilding glaze
Of same as primary-colour storms swirl
Across the West and blizzard-clumps amaze
April, while here poincianas unfurl
Their first incandescent orange-scarlet flags
(Sighted this morn, hurrah!), we sit content
In accustomed azure with frosty mugs,
Furnished with all a body ought to want.

As charmed weather flows in through doors flung wide,
Huff, far-off hurricanes, here all is well,
Only a lingering thirst keeps me inside.
Sojourning south of winter may dispel
New England chill, as Frost could testify,
But shifts perspective, as he would have learnt,
Moating the world of work, so finally
Sloughed the siren, stopped coming, cleared his throat

Of tropic flora, as Stevens, with whom
He coincided, had, finding the isle
Too seductive, her perpetual bloom
Disposed to compete with his hard-won style,
His art's stone walls. And if I should contrive
Not to return, or rather, journey back
The better to uproot, pack up and leave,
Settle for good, would my run of rhyme-luck
Break as I lolled and sipped and deepened tan,
Soul's health and high craft's at length clean forgot,
Contrary to my great Provider's plan?
Another? Yes, I shall; why ever not?

HAPPY HOUR AT THE GREEN PARROT

Il distratto? Which Haydn symphony?
    No, looks more philosophic, hand to chin
Like a Michelangelo Medici.
    Not that I reckon him specialist in

Metaphysics. No more am I. My gaze
    Keeps north-starring the shroud-print Union Jack
His jeans crotch spread wide on the stool displays,
    Or unawares exposes. Losing track

I drink, but before the swallow eyes snap
    Back to attention. Yes, really quite like.
Diagonal stress-marks X a treasure-map,
    Vertical zipper flap well-worn turnpike,

But how account the horizontal line
    Threading the lot? A sexual metronome?
Sexy, for sure. His corner seat fronts mine
    Caddy to the bar's full-house hippodrome.

Perched like chess-pieces waiting to be played
    We kill pints with ocular cat-and-mouse,
That so familiar game this now so staid
    Old number once played to a fuller house.

That even evening I might be prospect
    For *cinq-à-sept* this heat-charged afternoon
Leaves all my mossy suppositions wrecked.
    Forget Turin! The miracle's this boon!

After so long without the faintest flicker,
    The mildest case of curiosity,
Queen's pawn plants smack on my clapped-out old ticker
    The fairy-kiss of possibility!

THE ROOSTER

Perpetual party baled mid-flight,
  By five I lie wide-eyed
And taste the lull of ebbing night,
  Suspended hush outside

Broken only by chanticleer
  In nigh hibiscus-tangle
Accosting day by no means near
  With his unholy jangle,

The gouge of his relentless call
  Insistently replayed
Like doubt-wormed testimonial
  Undoing the betrayed.

These raucous nuisances are dealt
  A gift sophisticates
Might envy, if we thought or felt:
  Before light agitates

The ocean six blocks east, before
  The first faint sign appears,
Seeking no sign, needing no more
  Than instinct, proud cock rears

Taut throat and volleys sun-salute.
  O gift surpassing good,
To pierce pitch-dark with beam acute,
  Prescient with dawn-laced blood!

A RESTRICTED PALETTE

In this haven of indulgence,
  Teased maze of sensual delights,
  Colour is king. In frenzied flights
Bougainvillea founts immense

Neon waves, pulsing tints attack
  From dawn to blowout blaze of sun.
  Where nothing grown or done
Can be corralled in black,

I strive to take just measure
  With charcoal, not in oils:
  How hard poor bridled pencil toils
To transcribe senses' pleasure!

Mere bravura, ought one say,
  Swording with one hand tied?
  Or technique in its pride
Attempting to convey

A dimension through entire
  Absence—sculptor's Parian brush?
  Or reluctance to arm blush
With freedom, energy, fire?

True Tropicals

There is a garden in my mind—
By heat-advisory confined
To library quarters I scroll sites
       For tropicals.

Polysyllabic colour booms
Through names transcribing gorgeous blooms
Which kiss defeated lips to rights:
       Lush labials!

Calathea, Plumeria,
Zingiber, Heliconia—
Plumed images array the screen,
       Crammed catalogues

Looming an arabesque brocade
Even today's sun could not fade,
Until, gorged on what eye hath seen,
       Mind's stretched eye fogs,

Leaving day-dreamt sketch incomplete—
A land of reliable heat
That does not flare fierce and recede
       By giddy turns,

Where sun is a friend, not a god
Brandishing triple-digit rod,
Who, apprised what exotics need,
       Steadily burns.

Eager as I fever to raise
These corporeal fireworks displays,
It would be foolishness to tempt
       Such to unfold

In semblable tropics, pour forth
Freely, forgetful how far north
Lies this land seemingly exempt
        From killing cold.

The frame whereon to elevate
Coaxed blooms to images' estate,
Planting their tender roots in soil
        Warm as a nest

Is no dream, if settling there be:
A tropic sunset, floating free
Of fear of cold to delve and moil
        In charmed Key West!

Seize the dream! With apologies
To Aunt Jane, whose elegancies *
Such heat would shrivel to a swatch
        Of dimity—

At this late stage all I should choose
Would be beseech and bless the Muse
And cultivate my six-yard patch
        Of true frost-free.

* Jane Austen famously disparaged her work as "the little bit (two inches wide) of Ivory on which I work with so fine a Brush, as produces little effect after much labor."

PREVAILING CURRENTS

Thrall to steady trades, arboreal Quakers,
  Across the key palms' eyebrow-arched fronds wave,
Lapping blue-yonder like undulant acres,
  Soothing the restless medium they lave.

Sun scatters speckles as files pitch and roll.
  I watch their shadows languidly assault
A lattice, then a lush original
  As lazily caress the azure vault,

And bask content as furthest memory
  Can muster, plaguing cares sealed fathoms deep,
Save fear those trade-strophes seep into me
  And lull my artistry to unthrift sleep.

At Fort Zachary Taylor Park

For it is a ghost's right,
His element is so fine
Being sharpened by his death,
To drink from the wine-breath
While our gross palates drink from the whole wine.

      —Yeats, "All Souls' Night"

So palpable this pristine morn your shades
I move to mid-bench to make room for you,
Then recommence bestowing accolades

On the prospect's varieties of blue,
Sky, Gulf, Atlantic imperceptibly
Merging in greater good the home-key hue,

Supping perfect peace, smiling out to sea
This rare vernal pause in the Southernmost,
Then updredge, hooting the absurdity,

Yeats' Nobel speech (I who never engrossed
So much as a cereal-packet prize)
Invoking *his* shaping shades, both now lost

But ever-vivid to visionary eyes—
My pattern reversed, a brilliant young man
Whose gift Death shrank to minor-master size,

Old lady tottering past Biblical span
In a foreign body and age. Ah, we
Might have knit trio no less soul-wed than

Giants conjured in Stockholm—yes, we three
Might have smiled here together ... But we *do*,
You live in me as much as what *is* me—

And from first sight the bond between you grew:
Had freak or ailment claimed me, son claimed late,
You would have bridged the void, cradled her through

Years she would not have wanted, desiccate
Decades, and best-cherished hours would have been
Shared in silence like this, that happiest state

When words are surplus, thought-speech flows between
Fused hearts. And further up this right-hand sea
At her beachfront, sharing the aqua sheen,

Mother would turn come noon to ask of me,
"Time yet for a Bloody?" Darlings, high time,
Let us adjourn to some quaint hostelry

To sport in fanned shade, and squeeze the odd lime—
A summons none of our sort would refuse,
Condign precaution in this febrile clime—

And put ghost-trio silence to good use,
Wine-breath your portion, mine gross-palate brew,
Lavishing capital memory accrues
As all right-thinking wordsmiths haste to do.

An Ordinary Twilight in Key West

Why am I passionate about this place?
  Tonight teems with reasons more numerous
    Than foolscap legal's lines. Flame hibiscus
Blossoms blithely bobbing in sky's pale face
  Cypher relief the day's relentless heat
  Retires at scent-stirring rise of so sweet
A breeze as asperges twilight with grace.

Meridian cast no less complete a spell,
  Epiphany the last thing on my mind
    As I fled down Duval, a sweat-chequered hind,
To the next air-conditioned citadel:
  A cross-street sidewise glance flung my spent way
  Taut white sky's baked enamel purpling grey
Like the nacreous dome of an oyster-shell—

Stern and unsmiling as Byzantine Christ
  The tints framed a face for pitiless heat,
  Its triumph over my limp likes complete,
Proclaiming every bauble has been priced,
  Each honeyed hour of verandah repose
  Is writ for *Dies Irae* to disclose;
Not that such pleasures need be sacrificed,

But that they count for sin if not employed
  To fuel idle hands for worthy tasks.
  Not Byzantine but Puritan unmasks
That minatory sky—ah, how avoid
  Acknowledging the stern strain's primacy,
  The hard shibboleth of utility
Hissed by sea-captains who never enjoyed

Breeze for its own soft sake, but wondered where
    Their argosies were calmed, who ledgered coins
    Ignoring tropic stirrings in their loins
Save to increase themselves, wasted no care
    On aught but God and Mammon, one of whom,
    A Warwick Greene, immarbled waited Doom
Till hurricane surge clawed the south point bare.*

His name was—Pardon! A fit Christian to quell
    Storm and soften anger, roused sinner's plea.
    I tilt my glass to consanguinity,
Amendment of life, my prayer-book seashell
    Murmuring pardon and peace, pardon and peace.
    Rhode Island sire, may this amended breeze
Refresh your scattered bones. Here all is well.

* Pardon Greene (1787–1845) was a descendant of Dr. John Greene of Warwick,
Rhode Island, one of the founders of Providence. He was one of three New England
partners with whom John Simonton subdivided Key West, which he had purchased
in 1822. The great hurricane of 11–12 October 1846, worst in the island's settled
history, completely destroyed the burying-ground on the southernmost point;
body-parts, shrouds, and bones were left dangling from mangled trees.

V. LOVE'S LABOUR'S LOST

Berowne: O we have made a vow to study, lords,
And in that vow we have forsworn our books:
For when would you, my liege, or you, or you,
In leaden contemplation have found out
Such fiery numbers as the prompting eyes
Of beauty's tutors have enrich'd you with?

—*Love's Labour's Lost,* act IV, scene iii, lines 318–323

THE JOY OF COOKING

The last few heave-ho times, I must confess,
Were not chalked up unqualified success.
As I wince through passion's motions, pretending
Tooth for this custom-creased farce, mind's descending
To the larder to take in hand an onion,
Stripping crisp skin and membrane for extinction—
The sheer joy of fine dicing, worthy aim
Of adding zest to mélange, pot to flame,
Baking dish for hours while aromas tease
Cook settling into Crow-time's douce release:
Miles more congenial than love's shriek-believe,
Hurricane-heaves one were as lief achieve
Sniffing gamey milk. At length grown secure
In singlehood, I much prefer the pure
Purposeful motion of chopping-board knife,
Content to make an evening, not a life,
Fine dining, not hot lovers, to extol.
You heard the one about the casserole?

The Assistant Rugby Master:
A North Country Idyll

For T. A.

Old passion out to pasture twenty years,
How come you prancing back to pace forecourt?
Half-registered in sleep, last night's high winds
Must have blown down, with the usual fronds,
Fences in mind's policies, for I hurt
Today with pristine pain as love's dust stirs.

Temptress-victim of grand climacteric,
Sexual meltdown at sixth heptennial,
Suitor ne'er wooed so recklessly as you!
Crabbed wife passed out down the hall, you played through,
Proffered my lips the only glass still full,
Your fever-ripe flesh—and I blocked the kick,

Or dropped the pass, in parlance of the game
We coached together, helpless to control
Our fast-evolving match, neither much good
At this brave new contact sport of oeillade,
Changing room cat-and-mouse, stud of the hill,
Heedless of blowing jobs to dole-queue come.

As well, historic flame, all came to naught,
Though at the crash you would not understand,
And, overcompensating, ran into
Opportunistic clutches of a shrew
Worse torment than your first. At first, I planned
Breakaway love-neuk in Fife—overwrought,

Standing ready and thrilling to become
A martyr for true love, to be refused
Invitations to great houses, forfeit
Holyrood levées where footmen were not
Mere props of fiction, and the glasses raised
Spheres above what one decanted at home.

But ah, as you kept gym at some fifth-rate
Comprehensive, and charms fizzled, loaf brain
Wrinkled no whit nearer fathoming mine
Could we have guyed ourselves this love divine
Still excelled, might we have sustained a strain
Surely for braver hearts than ours too great?

Contorting to pass you for nonpareil
When at most the makings of one hot night,
Braw set of tackle, startling sapphire eyes—
And heart-snagging dependency I chose,
One season, to pronounce the sovereign note.
Dumb darling, it would not have done at all,

As David, whiskies deep, endured me spilling—
Love would have devolved in life without parole,
But cowardice not sense bade me deflect
Your ten-pint hand thrust forward to direct
Mine to present pleasure—stuff long-term goal!
What filled us then could not have kept fulfilling.

What do I wish for you? That no tempest
Bear snatches of my implausible peak,
That you sleep sound beside the second spouse,
Convinced each kiss she was and is best choice,
That I—there, spite of hope, you tongue the wrack
Of life-reversing passion long since lost,

Our might-have-been that never should have been.
Shall we shake hands on that? Ah, now I feel
That hand, plump, roughened as a plasterer's,
And yet—yet it held treasure that yet stirs
What's left of my heart, love stubbornly real,
Magic that has not visited again.

Reasoning it all wrong has done no good:
Blind heart, persistent in tombed heresies,
Believes it might have worked out after all.
When the path was never blazed, who can tell?
As on that threshold night, let us part ways,
I to heft pen, your empty hands to bed.

A Stingray in the Boudoir

What could possess the most *outré* of queens
   To site plate-front the *haut*-trash likes of *that*?
Presumably aimed at the queen of means
   Whose boudoir-buzz has gone a trifle flat,

Well-angled to entice the *louche* eye of
   An afternoon drunk lurching Duval's length—
Emblem of outrageous power, *très*-tough love,
   Hovering on stick above its plexi-plinth

Like the world's most disastrous canapé.
   What loser would lug home, or pay to ship,
A larger-than-life polymer stingray?
   Mauvais gout, nouveau riche, joined at the hip.

Then again, mightn't it help while the gap
   Between upright ape and carnal abandon?
Strategic fore-chat point, if total crap,
   Something to steady a verbal hand on

While glands are revving. Extract the *plastique*,
   Assist in civilization's downfall!
Pronounce the opportunity unique
   And swallow the staggering tag. Then drawl

In the pause-ridden down-spiral to sex,
   "*Etes-vous amusé*? Sort of a malign
Portabello—reminds me of my ex.
   That's my last duxelle on the wall..." No sign

Of clicking allusion? Doubtless he's quicker
   With bare hands. At least he's not polymer—
Add a little chat and a lot of liquor,
   Pièce de résistance is sure to stir.

An Absence of Aubade

Chanticleer's negative,
  I spatter pre-dawn hush
With harsh recitative,
  The cough I cannot shush

Nor palliative assuage,
  Startled awake to find
Longing, as not this age,
  For a roused sleeper's hand

Stroking my shoulder-blade
  As I prop arm to rise,
Sharer shaking fair head,
  Opening high-noon eyes,

Love's waking glance sure-shot,
  That momentary touch,
The right notes I hit not,
  More eloquent than speech!

Before I can ransack
  Remembered dawns' dream-hoard
To serve the present lack,
  The moment has expired,

I stumble to numb feet
  To limp renewed thread through
Maze mined with options shut,
  Schooling heart to make do

When no donor touch stirs,
  Or demigod descends,
With such song as occurs
  To my cracked ring-reft hands.

THE ARM OF FLESH

The arm of flesh will fail you,
You dare not trust your own.
                    —George Duffield

Will fail. Eheu. So I was warned, and so
Sung, E-flat hymn-ground crumbling in my hands
And bass at house prayers, many ports ago—
Bibulous foppish prime at which I blush,
Chaos of stymied ambition and glands—
And have proved fit for Thomas in my flesh.

Unlike the next-stool arm this happy hour
Tank-top material I never ranked
Even when smooth and slender in bright blur
Of vermeil youth. No hint of failure there—
Triumph of tan and tone, treadmill be thanked,
Perfection beyond reason as compare.

Those curves revert to Seicento chalk.
Apotheosis in a Baroque vault
Apart, how does one (say we) walk the walk
Of sovereign beauty? What's its earthly use?
Transfer-square the study, then scratch to halt,
At a loss to tong the coal while it glows.

The soupçon I boasted was never used
Save to quake a few shallow hearts, but this
Wonder at my elbow, looking confused—
Filling an application, I now see—
With honey-dripping biceps such as those
Should be applying for a Caracci

Who would grid the curves, then oil the outline.
Chalk, lick, touch, chip marble, whichever route
We choose, naught keeps the human form divine
And breathing, the Pygmalion in us strives
To charm the image back from finished art
To something we might hold, to flesh that lives

As we live and hunger. Aye, hold's the rub!
We murder to perfect, and straight unwish
Our artifice, of which today's ephebe
Seems innocent. Cursed with his pearl's price,
What could he do but flaunt that glowing flesh,
Or peddling, set it in the foil of vice?

Cheapened by use, yet rendered absurd
By mere being, how is beauty to be
And do? What need? Grant flesh its own reward,
Fleet sun of radiance with no regrets,
Solid and spirit and reliably
Surprised by horizon's slice when it sets.

VENUS AND JUPITER

For R.

Celestial experts peddle upbeat doom,
  Urging groundlings to scan the small-hours sky
    While time remains to catch the grand display—
Aeons will wane ere this pair tease night's gloom
  With their near-miss conjunction. You and I
    So called in plantations' halcyon hey-day
Would have been a field-hand "item," as we
In leaner times were once assumed to be.

Typically missing the *fête*'s apogee,
  The major *frisson* when they almost merge,
    Today I caught up with the dazzling pair
In pre-dawn pause of hushed expectancy,
  And read them without spectacles or mage
    (So bright they seemed to singe the passive air),
Straining to wheel back to the night they shone
Almost—how crude the naked eye!—as one.

Well-missed, this once, in view of the contours
  Of our *histoire*: The planets square as we,
    Twin dazzlers in our social firmament,
Once stood, my lethal beams engaging yours
  At duel-distance, coiled in casuistry
    Of motive and desire, still innocent:
One pair of brown come-hithers summoning
Their mirror, terrified the trap might spring.

Now planets blazon our somber story:
  Across a hundred drawing-rooms, just so—
    Spectre of masquerade, rout, oyster-roast,
Rockville piazza, then, most wrenchingly
  (Knowledge after we cease to wish to know),
    You, ignorant I'd washed back on this coast,
Spied at our old distance my grizzled head

Across a churchyard loamed with kindred dead.
Eye-searing you blazed with all the allure
  Of unsullied prime—display born of fear,
    Or justification, or mere reflex?
Of the answer's importance I was sure,
  Speaking as it did to motive, and clear
    Whatever else was murkily complex,
The years, for all my evident decay,
Had taken nothing of your power away.

Now grizzled both, aping the heavenly pair
  We trace respective orbits through the vault
    Of time allotted, sometimes meeting, yet
Never together, nor free to declare
  Passion we can neither prosper nor fault—
    Till Death part, and one mourner, features set,
At last approaching, bows grey head above
The waxen counterfeit of only love.

THE POLYPHONIST AND THE PEDERAST: TWO FARRANTS

Call to remembrance, O Lord, O Lord. *

Life dare not lift a candle to such art!
  Straining to keel my voice's bursting rapture
Steady on the stately stride of my part,
    Against the grain memory veers off into
    A second subject, namesake I once knew
When I was young and arrogantly pure.

In stanzas Ad. Lib. *compare and contrast*
  These unlikely name-mates divided by
Four centuries and light-years of zeitgeist.
    Hearing siren music, both seek a way
    To bid that impossible sweetness stay,
Snatching perfection from mortality.

Both hunger after beauty, yet for one
  The impulse ripples outward, speaking to
As needs be through strange tongues, sharing his passion
    Naked for all to read in cleft and stave,
    Swimming in waves of sound down a hushed nave,
Rivaling chancel-glass in rainbow hue.

T'other can only watch and wait and drool,
  Foraging guilt-sodden transports among
Changes and chances of a boarding-school:
    Warily working inward, he must hide
    From wife and colleagues his dark-of-moon side—
Madness to trust another living tongue.

So little culled for such a length of days,
  A waste of shame to garner briefest bloom,
And not a hope of the sweet meed of praise:
    Sterile career contriving pitiful
    Trysts in the showers—high bliss in towel's fall!—
Or staged encounters in a changing-room.

Traffickers both in the ephemeral
  Constellation of blent parts' unison,
The elder's manuscripts nearly as frail
    As offshoot's remembrance. Not much survives
    Of Farrant's oeuvre, but how that fragment lives
  To soar and shame a degenerate son,

His treasure trusted to singers who know
  To release, not to caress the rare note;
But for my era's Farrant, disjunct echo
    Of distant sire, hoarding is all he knows,
    His brief encounters stashed like dirty clothes,
  His song of rapture fit for no clean throat.

For this starved prisoner of pent desire
  By fleshly full-score bodies are obscene,
The apples of his ravenous eye retire
    Muscled, hirsute, mid-teen—blasted beauty
    Like a missed entrance, or basses' botched B
  Snapping the chord in measure seventeen.

* The opening words of the best-known anthem by Richard Farrant (ca. 1525–1580),
a Gentleman of the Chapel Royal of Edward VI from 1552, and under Elizabeth I
from 1564 Master of the Choristers at St. George's Chapel, Windsor. In 1569 he was
appointed to the equivalent position at the Chapel Royal, continuing to hold both
posts until his death. His surviving compositions are almost exclusively liturgical.

JUST BEING FRIENDLY

Die dumb-ass ist die allerbeste ass—
　　To hijack a Bach cantata. I' faith *
'Tis too often the case, and once more was
　　This happy hour passed next a five-star youth,

Votary to the screen above the bar,
　　Attending with groans of orgasmic glee
The toils of a bull-dyke pool-avatar,
　　Who'd hazard Yeats a truck accessory,

But was passing fair! Let me count the ways—
　　Shot-silk brown hair cascading from full crown
On atavistic English-schoolboy face:
　　The prefect with a heart. My eye worked down

To the bare forearm bordering my pint:
　　Flawless alabaster smooth as a boy's
Embellished with white-blond hairs' glinting lint.
　　A complicit glance brought me to face eyes

Beyond hyperbole—the rarest blue,
　　Not sapphire nor cobalt nor Nordic ice,
Somehow partaking of each jewel-hue,
　　Iris augmented by a bonus slice—

Supernal treasures wasted on the box
　　But not my pair pocketing without right:
Sockets waxing with brows' emphatic flex
　　Capri-caves shimmering with bouncing light.

He took me for a fellow son of sport
　　Bound to share his proprietary joy
In cue-armed dykes. Dévoté of a sort,
　　Indeed, but far from his flavour, poor boy.

If attentions might have converted me,
   Triumph his who drew me into the game,
Glancing, touching with radiant energy—
   But ace or duff, her shots were all the same

To one preoccupied: those dazzling eyes
   Fit to argue before Apollo's court
Too dim in worldly ways to recognize
   That for his latest mate they were the sport!

As slender fine-boned hands italicized
   Enthusiasm all about my body,
Returning pat for pat I temporized
   Right of reply: It almost seemed more duty

Than pleasure to keep his illusion whole.
   At last our heroine lost her endless match—
Nothing for it now but to console
   Him hug for hug. He consulted his watch,

Drained his glass, and with farewell ox-yoke hug
   Was gone, I thought, but turned and shook my hand,
Exiting with a glance and parting shrug
   I could not read. Why try to understand?

Smart girls don't mess with Greek gods—poor old Leda,
   Remember? Single mother saddled with twins.
Savour and let it go. Might as well linger
   A trauer-pint. Sometimes the loser wins. **

Pool's poetry? Don't be ridiculous—
   What daft delusion has occluded you?
You know he wasn't being serious.
   Ah, but his beauty was. If he but knew.

* The cantata BWV 106, *Gottes Zeit ist die allerbeste Zeit* (God's Time is the
Most Appropriate Time) of ca. 1707–1708, written for a funeral.
** German for "mourning."

THE STUD NOT TAKEN

For M. C.

Surprise-ensnared when handed one today
   By the hambergère's charcoal-flamed cashier,
I chewed my début turn as Cupid's prey—
   Prey's quarry, rather: Many and many a year
Ago to our seaside club came to play
   Just the fresh talent we'd hoped might appear—
A local school-leaver with failsafe hands,
Arresting speed and brawn—and rampant glands.

O times!—the greenest third-string flanker fell
   Like Lucifer for a fast-fading prop
No wise apprised he'd cast a fatal spell.
   Poor neophyte! The pass he couldnae drop,
But the stylus he wielded nae sae weil—
   Quite the wrong game-plan, placing atop
The till, where, that week's steward, I'd be sure
To register, the wages of allure.

Store-bought, with massed candy-pink hearts outside,
   And, proffered in chubby loops, yours within—
A schoolboy hand ripened body belied.
   Seldom had blazed into aesthetic ken
So pure a type of manhood reified
   As might tempt hardened ascetics to sin—
Michelangelesque, yet ruddy of hue:
Contours aside, naught marble about you.

Declaration had already been made
   At practice, in the showers, as across
Changing-room bench and clubhouse you betrayed
   Triumphant after scoring the pharos
Strobing searchlight of your lust. What delayed
   Comprehension, left me long lurched at loss
To read your kind attentions' true intent,
When body-language soared so eloquent?

If love-avowals of their nature shake
    Absurd fruits into laps, and own as much,
Yours was not humdrum gland-propelled mistake,
    Partook of the heroic, and as such
Befitting, seeing you were (apply the brake,
    Blanche, don't talk dirty, don't you dare to touch...!)
Out- and up- standing in other respects;
All roads ramble back to questions of sex.

Ah, how could I have been yours, or you mine?
    Disparity discounted, manifest
Absurdity, where does love form a line
    In passion's quicksand? At least you expressed
What your heart felt, while—craven, suave, benign—
    I never answered your appeal, that guessed
Would have curtained your rugby-club career
(Officer and gent, I'd have floundered clear).

Affirmation hid in my covert gaze
    Memorizing what I would not be getting,
Safe in the neuk we would not set ablaze,
    Little guessing how long I'd spend regretting
My reply untendered, our unseized days,
    Beweeping those beauties once so besetting
Subsumed in years and surplus flesh. Be mine?
O Valentine!—I'm yours in Eighty-nine.

A Waxing Moon

In the flat calm of an unfellowed night
  Sensing some shift, I rouse to find there gleams
A two-edged blade of beeswax-candle light
  Nigh the dark couch I share now but with dreams.

I trace the luminous shaft to its source,
  Flung casement through which a waxing moon sails
Serenely set on her westerly course,
  Beneath whose sterling smile the garden pales

To spectral day, its paltry landmarks pearled
  In that chaste light by which young lovers go
About their doomed delights, light of a world
  Remote from that we waning greybeards know.

An acorn's plosive fall I dream I stole
  Within its bound, rewound steps to apply
Heart's hard-won lessons to a body whole,
  Healed, confident, not with all sap sucked dry.

One cycle is our portion; mine is sped.
  With lingered Eden-quitting glance for speech
I turn to shadow and a narrow bed
  Pitched where full moon's tide will nevermore reach.

A GAIN:
EPITHALAMIUM FOR CHARLES AND RUTH PRICE

(16 April 2005)

First faint-edged songs are far more flavoursome
Than bold declaration—solitary bird
Probing pre-dawn hush while laggards lie dumb.

So much speaking before the spoken word—
The handshake held a quickening beat too long,
The casual shoulder-tap tattoo that stirred

Something dead, made me arch to swell in song.
Good reason wanting for impulse or taps,
Questions crowd thick—surely I read that wrong?

Can it be? O doubtless not—but—perhaps
(Whispers amplified by heart's emptiness)...
And lack of practice means one misreads maps,

Disoriented by dearth of success;
And "maps" implies this has somewhere to go;
And "this" scents a we ... Then one night you press

Your warmth all along my side, and I know,
Or almost do: We are not in a crowd,
Nothing external shoves you to lock so,

So it must be—? I all but ask aloud,
Flagging a border that may not be sealed
As I pray in gusts, my braced being bowed,

You pluck courage to voice what chafes concealed
In proximate breasts, for I seize with dread,
And should need all banked bravado to yield.

Your hands fleet harbingers, you take my head
In which lit eyes have poured four measures full,
More than lungs can balance note, and instead

Of speaking draw it to touch yours, tip skull,
Kiss my crown, distilling all words might say
In one faint shock, ever so gently pull

My bent frame upright, and draw yours away:
I feel your mouth, poised lips a haven's quay
As bird-embroidered dawn flares into day

Complete my breathless "O"—O can this be?
Harbour claps my trembling skiff to a main,
And before I know what has swallowed me
I have clambered ashore to love again.

VI. OTHER WORLDS

My eyes brim with past evenings in this hall,
Gravy-spattered cloth, candles minutely
Guttering in the love-blinded gaze.
The walls' original old-fashioned colors,
Cendre de rose, warm flaking ivory—
Colors last seen as by that lover's ghost
Stumbling downstairs wound in a sheet of flame—
Are hidden now forever but not lost
Beneath this quiet sensible light gray.

—James Merrill, "After the Fire"

GRAVEYARD SCHOOL

For Charles F. Price

Hallowed ground both, a fieldstone-walled kirkyard,
Its sleepers sloping gently south and west
From Greek Revival temple-crowned hillcrest,
T'other boasting no pillared sanctuary,
Hill unwalled, with unhewn nature left be,
Just pine and poplar standing unfussed guard.

Leagues different in their modes of sepulture,
Parted four hours' drive, say, a dozen years—
Not so ill-sorted as at first appears,
For long after pious visits they yoke
To convey a notion that never spoke
Either then, but now scythes the dumb obscure.

We crept about with the slight scholar's stoop
Investing haunters of such layered places,
But where so many lay in shrouded stasis
Our emphasis was not on death at all.
None of these dead were ones we might recall
In other state: their "sure and certain hope"

Had been invoked before we guides saw light.
Now we strengthened bond with a chosen friend
By showing him the stones whence we descend,
Presenting him, as though affianced bride,
To these blind parents paired on their hillside,
Raising friendship to higher power, new height.

"Dead they are not, these dry bones live in me,"
Without resort to speech I seemed to say
To David, Charles to me. A landmark day!
Sights seen, indeed, novel country unsealed
To eyes scion had perfect faith would yield
Response to enhance the pilgrims' amity.

In both forefathers came through halts and twists
From Scotland, whose son David, at Fairview,
Apprised my kin were Cunninghams, sieved through
Ulster, said so yonder vista revealed:
Hillocks bubbling in copse and cross-stitched field—
Pure Ayrshire! A marvel how type persists

In land as sharply chiseled lineaments!
And yet the spot Charles shared was not Caithness,
Whence his Gunns voyaged—little could be less
Like than forest-furred peaks. But, now I think,
Disconnection forges an unseen link,
Perplexity debouches rounded sense.

Bound, autumns beneath the bridge, for Orkney,
David and I sought out my Caithness kin
And found the spot, worn stones snugly walled in,
The roofless ruinous Auld Kirk of Thurso
Where was christened George Farquhar, who would go
To Charles Town and beget, remotely, me;

Whose daughter, after George died for his king,
Would wed a kinsman of Nathanael Greene,
Under whom, in the conflict's clinching scene
At Eutaw fought Charles's Gunn ancestor,
Their tales twined in his novel nicknamed *Nor*;
Such a craze of connexions helixing!

Through me these unacquainted friends clasp hands,
David with Charles, who, many leaf-falls on,
Led to the river where his Scots had sown,
Seed of that Revolutionary sire,
Nothing like stark northmost cliff-gadrooned shire,
Like nothing I'd seen here or in far lands,

God's acre paced on high hill's balding pate,
Arboreal outworks ringing exposed dome
Where scores of warriors and farmers, called home,
Lay under markers struggling to maintain
Composure in the pitch of steep terrain,
Angled like revelers frozen in dram-spate.

Low quilted cloud-banks flinted phosphor-gleam
That lent the whole prospect a headstone cast
Painting enveloping stillness more vast.
A few pewter brush-flecks marked where below,
Through woods clinging to leaf, swift-footed Toe
Purled faint as vanished Alph after the dream. *

Hands bore their loved aloft that they might lie
Nearer Heaven, I heard, and in this way
Steal a march on cove-folk come Judgment Day.
Host become guest among ancestral bones,
Stirred by a skirl of tones and overtones
I blessed the friend who coaxed my steps so high,

Blessed both friends in that moment's charged release
For shoring heart's ruins with rock constancy,
Enriching my span immeasurably
Commingling their love and things loved with mine,
Hearkening my songs, honeying salt decline
Towards the long pause with fathers such as these.

* The South Toe River is formed in Yancey County, North Carolina from streams
draining the Black Mountains, and flows north to meet Crabtree Creek near Micaville.
Here it becomes the North Toe and forms the meandering boundary between Yancey
and Mitchell counties, flowing past the Johnson Cemetery at Toecane as it snakes
north and west towards Tennessee. Just before crossing the state line it joins the
Cane River to become the Nolichucky River. Alph is the "sacred river" in Coleridge's
visionary poem "Kubla Khan."

CONNECTING THE BOSSES

A drowsing cat curled round a shedding tree
Upholsters a piazza-pot's clay O:
A cathedral-vault boss (those High Gothic
Space-stations), or a pulsating Celtic
Emblem? A second eyeful whispers no:
No emblem there, but blessèd memory,

A loose-leaf file of mind's-eye images
Of just such swirling curves in chiseled stone,
Gordian love-knots of crisp artifice
Knitting a groin-vault's ridged ribs in precise
Progression. An age since I studied one
A hundred feet above my squinting eyes.

At Vickery's Bar I look up and behold
The inverse of scrupulous craftsmanship,
Galvanized ductwork snaking every which way,
Board game no one remembers how to play.
Mnemosyne, kind dame, suffers me slip
Back to church-haunting summer jaunts of old

When I culled images that now embellish
A much-diminished sphere. The other night
Friend boss-cat underwrote a Gothic fugue
As a well-lit dream chose to disembogue
In myriad passages whose rationed light
Kept me from threading them as one might wish,

But as I groped and gaped half-recognized
An aspect here and yon, a weird mélange
Of Wells and St. Andrews—the sky-roofed Pends *
Whose ribs break off like stalks as stone ascends
And halts confused—as I woke, feeling strange
And then with sunburst hindsight realized

I might have passed my golden years abroad
Needling architectural nectar, or
Quaffing real ale in pubs with beams above
My fuddling head, not ducts. Now as I move
Out of a setting-sun-shaft, and call for
Another half-price domestic, I read

Tart truth deferred, my titanic mistake
In limping home from Jamesian exile—
In a drought of morbid doubt I blinked, and
Repealing half a life sought my birth-land
To plant anew what flourished for a while,
Or seemed to, as I hoed old haunts to wake

The phantom vita nuova to fruit,
Till at length the once-pert seedling shriveled.
Could my heart survive another transplant?
The stalk would snap—I know, but do not want
To voice my answer. One more truth withheld.
No longer now a spruce wide-eyed recruit

But grizzled ghost, I never could succeed
In learning over all frail flesh forgot.
Sit tight and sip a cold one, baffled husk,
And dream of soaring through a Gothic dusk
Sloughing your crumbling flesh but somehow not
Ecstatic senses. That were vault indeed.

* On the edge of the cathedral complex at St. Andrews, a road runs from South
Street through what was formerly a vaulted chamber. This feature is known as The
Pends.

DREAMING OF SPIRES

Chamber walled shut, cast out of mind
  A century's cobwebbed abeyance—
Stale emptiness so long confined
  Rings change of air when sleight of chance,
  A hollow tap, reveals what once
Was centre of a living house;
  Shadows that cloaked great swathes for years
(Smaller our scale) abruptly choose
  To lift: A prospect reappears,
  Heart feasts on memory's arrears,
Leaving dazed mind a threshing-floor
  Heaped with uninvoiced husks of grain.
This morning a rubbled-up door
  Snapped seven seals, swung wide amain
  On tarnished trove that long had lain
Unmissed amid the fevered fret
  Of daily bread. Sun thrust a spear
Through heavens' six-scrim backlit set,
  Wintry clouds rare as snowfall here,
  Stray glance traversed a huge elm's bare
Ribbed sieve of a goblet, and Lo!
  A second rent—decades erase,
And out the vasty long-ago
  Another spire assumes the place
  Of the familiar flèche of Grace.

St. Mary the Virgin transferred
  To a land with no stone to cut
Or carve, looking faintly absurd
  Breasting a palm-frond tide, yet not
  So eye's mistake—for I forgot
Our White modeled his stucco spire *
  On the one that anchors the High.

About my head an Oxford choir
  Of images sings meltingly
  As through memory's gauze-veiled eye
I gaze on that spire from Boars Hill,
  Pinnacle blanched by summer sun,
Sheep-cropped pasture utterly still
  Save for brush-swish—a view begun
  In confidence, but far from done
Abandoned, as is not my wont
  But sometime way. From high-walled lanes,
Across the meadows, how they haunt,
  Refracted scenes, impaled remains,
  The quilt-scraps memory retains!

Now mind's eye pans to Selden End **
  Where my young-poet dreams dissolved
In antiquarian thirst to mend
  Cracked pedigrees so long unsolved
  The armorial puzzles once resolved
Seemed compensation for rich verse
  Left unstitched: the scholar's baby
Steps! Granted I might have worked worse
  With those hours; that delving taught me
  As much as dons of what would be
My most of life, dispensing light
  To students and through scholarship.
What youth ever got it all right?
  Glugging the wine he ought to sip,
  Eager to shine as prone to slip,
Squandering, repenting in haste.
  Not that I squandered my time there—
Is happiness ever a waste?—
  But that that byway led nowhere.
  I might have crafted a career,
Withered into recondite bloom,
  Wise in distinctive Oxon fashion,
Compounding knowledge in the room
  Of ordinary life, vulgar passion,
  Tilling one's patch to perfection.

Evensong at New—trebles soar, ***

Descant to sere dons' crabbed tunes.

Nowhere. Empty chamber. Sealed door.

Inscriptions' illegible runes.

In my house are many lagoons.

* Edward Brickell White based the spire of Grace Church, Charleston (consecrated in 1848), the city's first in the Gothic style, loosely on that of St. Mary the Virgin, the University Church of Oxford (ca. 1280).
** The west wing of Duke Humfrey's Library (completed in 1490), Selden End, whose interior fittings date from the reign of Charles I, is one of the most beautiful rooms in the Bodleian Library. Genealogies, parish registers, and county histories reside here.
*** New College has one of Oxford's three full choirs of adult choral scholars and boy trebles.

A Harvard Triptych

I.
Sappho in the Snow:
A Vignette from the Time of Troubles, 1969

To the memory of Professor Sterling Dow
(19 November 1903–9 January 1995)

A long night in Widener straining to squeeze
Sappho into resistant head and tongue:
By ten I'd had, if not quite conned, my fill,
And sought the Yard, where all was spectral, still
And starlit, night the old girl might have sung,
With Attic-black effects in snow-clad trees.

Awash in the Aegean, at the east gate
I was met, clubbed, cursed, kicked, knocked to the ground
By Boston's finest charging Quincy Street.
The armies of light melted in retreat.
Dribbling lip-blood and snow, I glanced around—
Not a soul in sight to commiserate.

On impact the unarmed poetess had flown
From trampled book-bag to grace a slush-bank.
Righting myself, hand to now-throbbing head,
Cold, wet, dazed, but thankful not to be dead
(Only a stick—it might have been a tank),
I revived with a comprehensive groan.

Next letter home would scramble emotions,
My far-famed skirmish outlive bump and cut:
Mother laughed for years at the missive sent
To advertise this shocking incident,
That pompously pronounced her son "somewhat
Amazed" by Blue Boy's fulsome attentions.

The experience might have recruited me
For some revolution, schooled me to curse
Authority that deals the guiltless terror—
But I chalked mistreatment to human error,
And, near-miss martyr for Greek lyric verse,
Took vocab and verbs more seriously.

II.

BREAKFAST WITH LOWELL

Quincy House, Harvard, dawn of Seventies:
After reading from the dining-hall stage
Last night our High Poet surfaced early
(For him) and takes the place opposite me,
Parsing his plate as though a new language,
Its tropes under construction. We knock knees,

I inch back my chair, smile at him, then frown
Through the pitiless plate-glass bordering
Our table on a courtyard still ice-glazed,
Bleak beyond belief, three years flown amazed
I'm not yet seasoned—by calendar spring,
But cased in cold Lowcountry's never known.

"Cousin Robert, that's an egg, remember?"
Apparently not. He eyes it askance,
Scapegrace lately reproved by a prophet.
"Trust me—quite good. Promise, you'll enjoy it!
We love them down home." His fork takes a chance.
"Come visit! April there, not December."

Chatting to chafe him to cheer or to wrath
At another callow larval A.B.
Worshipping the wreck of a major mind,
I coax him through bacon. He seems resigned
To this gauche young man's chirpy sympathy
(I'm glad we weren't kin to Sylvia Plath).

168

Not long back from the annual madhouse stint,
Flailing to re-enter the outer world,
He looks more detached than usual today,
Summons nothing magisterial to say
As his fork makes lace of the now congealed
Much-vaunted egg he shoots a wary squint.

Like me myopic, yet he saw beyond
Aught plate-glass frames into the very heart
Of the age whose laureate he became.
Fried egg? No, he couldn't quite place the name,
But tamed the sorrows that set him apart
In his swansong sonnets' slough of despond.

Imperishably great, the best will live
While language breathes, but these days I'm afraid
To touch them, that pleasure scarce worth the risk
Of catching their tenor, those basilisk
Songs hatched in the last death-shadowed decade
Less keen observers made shift to survive.

III.
THE GHOST OF LAWRENCE SUMMERS

> Draw round, beloved and bitter men,
> Draw round and raise a shout.

—Yeats, "The Ghost of Roger Casement"

> O what has made that sudden noise?
> What on the threshold stands?
> 'Tis righteous leftists trumpeting
> Harpies with fresh demands.
> Screw the serial apologist,
> What's left of manhood kick!
> Swear his off-the-record remark
> Made you "physically sick."
> *The ghost of Lawrence Summers*
> *Is bleating at the door.*

"Why should the search for truth impede
The tread of thought-police?
Let him who twisted our pantyhose
Pay the ultimate price,
Abdication crown his wretched reign!
 How dare he postulate
Alleged differences between
The sexes are innate?"
     The ghost of Lawrence Summers
     Is bleating at the door.

"We never should have stomached him—
Elitist snow-white prick
Who demanded scholarship from
A black academic,
Bucked the ideological tide—
Outmoded as Canute!"
The abject bastard hoofs stage-left,
Feminazis in pursuit.
     The ghost of Lawrence Summers
     Is bleating at the door.

I sat and wept beside the Charles,
Bewailing what's become
Of first-light Harvard, once so fair!
Safe-havened in the tomb,
My masters, Dow and Jackson Bate,
Rejoice you did not see
What has befallen all you loved,
And all you hoped might be.
     The ghost of Lawrence Summers
     Is bleating at the door.

SIZING THE CATCH

I.

As on nearly all the thousands of nights
  Of our long bi-continental divide,
  Keenly I wish you, *caro*, at my side
To share this *crépuscule*'s unsliced delights.

It curtains a day the refulgent double
  Of Breton Augusts half a life ago;
  Buoyant and young, we were blessed not to know
What crumbling years would bury in their rubble.

And this was ever our stock-taking hour.
  Vistas chalked, landmarks notched, at length we'd slack
  Pace, heavy with rapture, slowly curl back,
Having consumed all dazed eyes could devour,

Always, dreams tell, to the same charmed auberge,
  To the same *place*-commanding high cool room
  Lazily sketching what mouths would consume
When well-oiled appetite bade us emerge.

II.

As in joint ventures to other Celtic lands
  I would rest eyes and crooked back, you would fetch
  Grateful libations and the bright day's catch,
The watercolours fresh from happy hands,

Après pique-nique, by way of *digestif*,
  While you drowsed in high grass beside a moat
  Across which subject chateau seemed to float
Most benign of ghosts. This was joy in chief,

Reliving our day as we sized and weighed
  The impressions you always reckoned good
  And I wished better, sharper, knew I could
Improve *demain* on what today had made,

171

The all-potent yeast of your approbation
   Thrusting my art beyond itself, into
   New realms, each afternoon's frenzy-brushed view
Rising to match the pitch of expectation.

III.

The pictures that have lived to tell late tales
   Are of those interludes twixt day and feast,
   Those second fruitings when review increased
Gross estimate, and small-scale craft spread sails.

These pelican memories that flock to feed
   Verging senescence are substantial fare
   Though phantom seen wrong way. What should I care
I dwell with phantoms if they glove my need,

And stop shrill demons' mouths with olive-sprigs?
   But if—this day of rapt remembering,
   When sun swelled to summer, breeze stuck at spring,
And brushes danced their merriest old jigs—

If you were at my side to fill and raise
   Cups and marshal sketches, how they would fly
   Above all estimate! Were you but by
To vivify the harvest with your praise!

THE OCULUS

From a leaf-shadow-stippled deck I spy
   Through a million-note adagio of verdure
     An oculus piercing the forest-dome,
    Tulip and plagued-locust plaited aperture,
      And swim to the original in Rome
Through which I stared at white-hot summer sky,

Felt nothing, so returned to Raphael,
   Thence to Venice, for this circle's untrue,
     Oval now I examine the framed scene,
    Scudding cheek-clouds foot-racing on pale blue,
      I've seen there, a pocket of calm between
Frescoed Titans tumbling, lodged in cove-swell

Corner of some vertiginous sala,
   The route to which I trace, but not the name
     Of its palazzo above the Rialto,
    The calle-entrance surprisingly tame
      For what awaits—best guidebooks bade me go,
Pay, and pepper the air with "ooh" and "ah."

Why paste Venice on Appalachian sky?
   Good enough in itself, this land where cove
     Is wooded vale, not a transition-zone
    To Tiepolo gods in giddy love.
      Why cannot memory leave me alone
To live the present, former lives laid by?

Perhaps I never should have ventured east,
   Less spent half a life on the further side
     But quaffed my fill of sun-blessed Italy
    And fair northern lands from their plundered pride,
      Heaped art; books, engravings, photography;
Would thirst for own eyes' proof ever have ceased?

Re-grafted thirteen summers to these shores,
  Having known many-layered worlds I still
    Find this I homed to strangely incomplete,
  Never free-standing, always itch to fill
    Its gaps with Europe, faint-willed to defeat
Urge to refurbish from memory's stores.

As branches part to shower light leaves hid
  Unable as sunlight not to compete
    Fuller phases abroad break in and steal
  Present's thunder, leaving that where my feet
    Powder this tulip-leaf never quite real,
But always tethered to a ghostly grid.

CONLEY RIDGE

The updraft breeze renders each tulip-tree
A thousand palms lifted against the light
As though protesting its intensity

At this elevation where it feels right
To be—no Petrus I, but buy his hint, *
Transfigured by upwelling delight

To image improvised establishment
Honing at so great height a mind gone slack
To stretch perception to fullest extent,

Trace numberless ridges of mountain-back
Behind, beyond, as though I took charcoal
And plunged towards white with inspired attack,

Convinced of hand's main force as worthy goal,
Each ordered swell known like a well-thumbed love,
Rightness flaming the fibres of a soul

Caught up in the perfect assurance of
The Divine Draughtsman who in a sublime
Asymmetry of swerve, dip, peak, drop, curve

Ordained each line and bathed it in such light—
A Bruckner melody flowing past time
Or undulant sentence supremely right
Endlessly weaving out of sound and sight.

* In St. Matthew's account of the Transfiguration, "Then answered Peter, and said
unto Jesus, Lord, it is good for us to be here; if thou wilt, let us make here three
tabernacles; one for thee, and one for Moses, and one for Elias" (17:4).

AN UPPER ROOM

A Reading by Fred Chappell, John Ehle, Charles Price, and Isabel Zuber, Little Switzerland Book Exchange, 1 October 2005

Parlour bedecked awaiting plight of troth
Or obsequies; for expected empties,
A centre-table veiled in bolts of cloth.

My séance quip fleshes in strategies
The authors reach into locked long-ago
To touch the former selves who crafted these

Wonders they stitched and now but partly know,
In awe themselves of what their hands create,
Connecting with their audience, being so.

Two wrote for decades at prodigious rate;
The voices placed between these famous men
Unearthed their talents relatively late—

Like students who most of the hour poise pen
Then whelm virgin blue-books with themes gnawed free,
Racing to cheat proctorial "Amen"—

Pulsing with all the artesian energy
Of uncurbed youth, mining the past to make
Dimming backward present reality.

Snatch that table-veil! This is not a wake,
But marriage of minds in an upper room,
Vocal quartet with repertoire to slake

Even Cana-thirst—for miracles come
Freely pouring in interplay so fine,
Concord so perfect strained senses sink dumb;

These improvised notes amount to design,
A magic no one present understands—
And then the mystery dissolves in wine,

Sunlight, music on a porch that commands,
Like our stars, eagle views, who as they sign
Stroll with rapt friends through Art's far-fertile lands—
And every word exchanged is joining hands.

Edina Fair

Sun slopes aside as furrowed clouds knit brow
And drops begin to streak the path I take.
By lunchtime light and weather have conspired
To reproduce your sere aspect, as mired
In vexed tasks I marvel I could forsake
The loveliest of cities for this—how,

How on earth could I work such woe, and why?
Questions sigh to silence. Your triad name,
Cadence sounding footfall dying away
On road ill-chosen, haunts each dead-end day
Spent circling back to sup on same self-blame,
Rapt happiness' unfathomed wish to die.

Horse-chestnuts in Queen Street Gardens, a glimpse
Of gesso Fife, castle-scarp, fanlight-slice—
Your revenge is my haunting day and night
As stray tapestry-thread catches the light:
Why ever did I fling my pearl of price
Into the chilly murk of a past tense?

The other noon a seagull swooped to shriek
"Edina" accusingly as I smiled
On warmer waters, and the drops fought home.
Just now, most cruel tease, there seemed to come
A pipe-skirl, but I knew myself beguiled,
Music not near but decades back to seek.

If I return, it must be as a ghost
Misting the scenes of more melodious years
On your enchanted slopes—enchanting still,
But radiance no proof against the chill
Of wasted life poking through blinding tears
For the all-precious pearl some doomed fool tossed.

THE ALEXANDRIA LIBRARY

When at last I come to possess my own,
  Solicitors' snail-slime somehow endured,
And find house regained expectably strown
  With squatters' trash, and liberate all stored,
  Abrupt decision's hastily piled hoard,
Shall I come on any treasure unturned,
Deposits surviving those bridges burned?

What a drum-roll moment when I unlock
  The wine-cellar, or keyless, smash door wide,
With what gorgonian spectacle struck,
  What revenge of inanimates denied
  Light and air too long find jumbled inside?
Pulp, dust, rat-leavings, ancient mind-fires' ash,
My precious books, my Prosperonian stash!

I shall hinge wide my young mind like a trunk—
  Volumes from earliest Edinburgh days
As tale-saturate as village quidnunc,
  Each wrapped in its own history, every phase
  Alive in artifact—trembling trace
Purchase, place, how motley hungers aligned,
What aspirations stirred that yet green mind.

Voyages' coordinates circle back,
  Mark each world-widening classic's reign begun—
Inverleith Pond-side, Green Walk's glade-flanked track,
  Fickle Scots sun saluting knowledge won,
  Grass-stain, pressed leaf, blanched page, insect undone
Ambering the sessions by which mind's bow
Curved to the impress of latest hero.

Bottle-missives scrawled for a later self,
  Stranger who ranged over decades' deep seas,
Margin-jottings sound time's sundering gulf—
  Quaint chirps, burst jokes, dissensions, theories—
  No notion survives what to make of these;
Even the hand I scarcely recognize,
Slender and fey as the penman once was.

Most eloquent of all, no doubt, the point
  Where life interposed, or ascending mind
Stumbled panting, or love fell out of joint
  And I broke off, leaving the text behind
  For unimagined grandsire-son to find
And finish. But would it be wise to graft
A set mind's slip on trunk a young one left?

Perhaps the key were better left mislaid?
  Indeed books furbish life, being in turn
Depth-sounding charge and consoling gourd-shade.
  That door need be breached, if but to inurn
  Vestigial hopes I might one day return
To a fragment of the idyll enjoyed
When books sufficed to fill the spirit's void.

AFTER THE FIRE

"They shook their heads and sewed him up again."
  Those doomsday words, whispered as elders rocked,
Often shook my ears as I hunched within
    Earshot ignored, supposed too young to know
  Or care about their talk, securely locked
    In innocence—but only seeming so.

Cancer's number I had, that ate away
  Father before my eyes while I was four;
Of whom also I'd overheard them say
    Nothing remained to do but pray and wait
  And dilute pain; science availed no more.
    I pieced the truth that no one told me straight.

At least when Father suffered I was there,
  Crouched under chairs, behind tickling brocade,
No more in sight than mind, as all their care
    Anointed the guest who would soon depart,
  Learning a hard-edged word watching him fade
    Until one dawn the cancer found his heart.

Another dawn finds me five thousand miles
  From noon that rakes the ruins of my house,
Wrapped in thick darkness as memory compiles
    Lists of losses, compelled to navigate
  By nightmare vision, watching water douse
    Flailing flames, and so doing, saturate

Treasures fire and smoke neglected to rob.
  The house was sick. Perhaps it would have been
Kinder of those flames to finish the job,
    Make the clean break I never could persuade
  Myself to sanction. But what might keep clean,
    Muddied with so much of my life? Dismayed,

I see a muddled afterlife arise—
   Scorched, charred, soaked, but stubbornly harled and tiled, *
Its heart scooped out, as of the enterprise
     Long since, so far removed, too poor to make
   Repairs, set wear to rights. Now comes a mild
     Request from my solicitor to take

Necessary steps to have the hexed house sealed,
   Engage joiner (in those parts also still
Undertaker) lest the rudely revealed
     Riches within attract children, for whom
   I should be liable ... O unclean kill,
     Rather a pyre than this sieve of a tomb!

Board it up to dream of prosperous days,
   Hoping that before it succumbs to rot
Some knight with golden pockets comes and pays
     For privilege of salvaging the wreck.
   A tortured body cries to be sewn shut.
     I shake my head and authorize the cheque.

* As is typical of seventeenth- and eighteenth-century houses in coastal Fife, mine had harling (a form of roughcast) applied to the stone walls, and was roofed with Dutch pantiles.

THE IDEA OF WALLACE STEVENS AT FETTES COLLEGE

For My Scholars

> Out of this same light, out of the central mind,
> We make a dwelling in the evening air,
> In which being there together is enough.
> —"Final Soliloquy of the Interior Paramour," ll. 16-18

Poured out like water, as the scriptures say,
    Or pints of cask-conditioned 80 / :
I mostly lapped the latter in my day,
    My Edinburgh prime devoted to filling
Finest young minds with what I came away
    From years of fancy schooling without spilling.
With Upper VI, my labour's chief delight,
Shared pints irrigated Orphic insight.

Ripest of all was summer term, when we
    Convened to prep for the A-Level "A"
Certain to boost, if not quite guarantee
    A shot at Oxbridge, goal none might gainsay,
Validating five years' starred industry
    Vaulting top-notch bar to strut it Sir's way,
At the Omphaloi to continue inhaling
Spice-land clouds of allusion he came trailing.

Suspicion whispers it shared illusion
    That I *taught*—I saw the syllabi through,
But teaching was more properly infusion
    Of passionate allegiance to a few
Exalted names, notes towards a prolusion.
    Of the great I eagerly led them to
No name, even Yeats', outshone that of Stevens,
The elect pole-star of my metrical heavens.

Just as well he was never a set book
  With its closed agenda of urgency.
Approaching his verse, we were free to look
  And leap at will, to splash excitedly
In fancy's fountain—how that class-shed shook
  With their close reading's *demonstrandum* glee!
I assured he'd help them learn how to think—
Goal from which modern "educators" shrink.

Most of the lines we read I understood
  Unsettlingly little better than they;
That as pilgrims we were equals was good
  I came to see as we puzzled pursed way
Through the "Auroras" in a brotherhood
  Of bafflement, straining to hear him say
Something we might hammer into rough sense,
If not the jewels he meant to dispense.

They were catching me up, and sometimes out.
  Given a few more years, they would possess
All knowledge I then stored—fair turn about,
  Mine any parent's self-blotting success,
Equipping his nestlings to soar without
  Precept or example, becoming less
The more absorbed. Dominie's Totentanz,
Piping himself towards irrelevance.

Much of Stevens continues to elude.
  I love no less the "Notes" lately reread
Than in far prime, but, obliged to conclude
  I follow no more nimbly, shake my head.
Yet collapse of a sense of certitude
  Beginneth wisdom—so I often said
To my charges: beyond, beneath, beside
Answers is where prime truth tends to reside.

A green leaf spiraling through Lothian sun,
    The last of these sessions moors in my mind:
Pitching our airy scholars' pavilion
    Before the cricket score-hut, unconfined
By walls, desks, or revision left undone,
    We staked a dappled patch where they reclined
As I played cross-legged prophet, a pitched stone
Circled by ripples it might boast its own.

I read to them, my voice the only gloss,
    Inflections, pauses, all the hints I gave,
Those strange late lyrics of triumphant loss,
    Crumbling body rapt singing could not save,
Mind sloughing its own muscle as mere dross,
    Plunging beyond itself in wave on wave
Of abstract ecstasy ... And there they lay,
Real and present as the warm June day.

My scholars! Glancing up at stanza-break
    I met their bodies scattered on the grass:
Accomplished, fully ripe fruit, equipped to slake
    All lower thirst, yet in another class
Those supple minds, where much was left to make,
    That, if my wishes for them came to pass,
Would swell to such raptures as awed flesh dumb,
Yet dwell in easy equilibrium

A time, till body crossed the great divide,
    Began trickling downhill, freeing up mind,
Chip of the central orb he reified,
    Mica-fleck flash, to leave safe slopes behind,
Climbing higher and higher, casting aside
    All not itself, at length coming to find,
Satisfaction no doubt-worm dare destroy,
It needs no ground to tread save its own joy.

Then they would know what I had sought to do
    When they were young. As our swan-session waned
I read the planet poem, tapering to
    The vivid sense of ending that now reigned
In circling hearts, to bow adagio through
    The "Final Soliloquy." What remained
When all was flown or blown? They did not need
Be told that question was the lyric's seed.

Stevens said more than all I meant to say
    In eighteen lines of overlapping lulls,
Where maker and made merge at ebb of day
    And stout heart from encroaching silence culls
The verdict with which mind tiptoes away
    From art divinely wrought, two syllables:
"Enough." It was; each valedictory eye
Welled tears awaiting work would not soon dry.

THE WILD SWANS AT CELLARDYKE

For S.C.F.

Of how many memories might I swear
Not just to drift of speech, who hammed which part,
How set and lighting spoke, but month and year?

As few, I trow, as loves that scorched my heart.
In September of the year of disgrace—
Suffer the number sleep—I oiled the smart

Of hurt a month of moons would not erase,
Summer foolishness ripened to a tone
Not to be reproduced, forfeit of face—

For love, as I averred. That year's heat was done,
You were back at school, our seasonal folk
Shuttered weeks since. And soon I would be gone,

Back to Edinburgh to resume my yoke,
Ploughing virgin tilth of scholars. Each morn
Sun slipped a little further off his stroke,

Slower, seeding less sheen. Widowed, forlorn,
I paced sour wait in spyglass oriel,
Deaf to savage strictures of self-scorn.

As witching approached burnt-out heart would swell,
With what I could nowise name, then at last
You sauntered down the brae and cast your spell,

Nor once met my gaze as you profiled past,
Though surely my hopeless vigilance screamed.
Eyes tugged the westering shadow you cast

187

Ambling the shore-hugging wynd till I dreamed
Mystic cloud swallowed you, not townward turn,
Despairing how the day might be redeemed,

Asking how long extinguished love could burn.
I looked between the harbour's outstretched quays
Where glided in with sovereign unconcern

A single swan, image designed to ease
Hours clouded by the mess fool heart had made.
Not before had I counted one of these

Fair creatures here, nor would a lean decade
Behold his like. He seemed to fan a wake
Of tonic calm. I was swift to persuade

Myself he swam as symbol, but what make
Of the message? You metamorphosed, come
Back to vanishing point to bid me take

Comfort, bind up wounds? My head was too numb
To decipher, the season had expired,
I headed south, work weaned me from those glum

Self-pitying postures, soon enough mired
In Michaelmas, and when holidays came
Bringing return, my symbol had retired.

You were about, your beauty shone the same—
Yet not, for I felt with shuddering start,
Though less to my comfort than transposed shame,

The months had after all patched up cracked heart.
Now, that beauty eclipsed, gone with the hair
I trembled to touch, we bide worlds apart.

Word comes of reprise of that vision rare,
A lone swan in our harbour (ours by right
Of the ancient drama enacted there),

Bearer this time not of balm or delight
But dread plague, dead, mauled, beached on the slipway,
The lead disaster of *World News Tonight.* *

A symbol yet? Though I cannot gainsay
Love's banded swan, your still correlative,
Is as dead, I hope deciphered it may
Infect us not to languish but to live.

---

* The BBC *World News* on the evening of 5 April 2006 began with the startling
announcement that a wild swan found dead on the slipway of Cellardyke Harbour
in Northeast Fife on 29 March had tested positive for the H5N1 strain of avian
influenza, the first confirmed case in Britain. The ensuing media frenzy made the
quiet village of Cellardyke briefly a venue of global interest.